More Praise for *The Shareholder Action Guide*

"*The Shareholder Action Guide* empowers every investor to work with corporations to be part of the solution. This is a must-read to help mobilize a shareholder movement that will have a major impact on climate change and other critical issues of our time."
—**Timothy E. Wirth, former US Senator (Colorado) and Vice Chair, United Nations Foundation**

"With practical information and compelling accounts of how shareholders are pushing corporations to improve their conduct, *The Shareholder Action Guide* is a must-read for investors mystified by the proxy process yet eager to align their assets with their values."
—**Fran Teplitz, Executive Codirector, Green America**

"*The Shareholder Action Guide* is an incredibly important and timely reminder of what each of us can do to challenge corporate and CEO misconduct. It's a must-read for anyone looking to influence how companies treat their employees and our planet."
—**Eugene "Rod" Roddenberry, President and Director, The Roddenberry Foundation**

"Both a historical primer on the movement's founders and a practical how-to manual, *The Shareholder Action Guide* demystifies the process of shareholder advocacy for concerned investors looking to catalyze enduring social and environmental change through the management of their investments."
—**Joshua Zinner, CEO, Interfaith Center on Corporate Responsibility**

"This inspiring work empowers shareholders, both large and small, to hold corporations accountable. These incredible stories of shareholders who have made real change are a powerful call to action."
—**Ben Cohen, cofounder, Ben & Jerry's, and Head Stamper, Stamp Stampede**

"I have been involved in shareholder advocacy for over forty years. I don't think I have seen such a thorough presentation in one place of its nuts and bolts. *The Shareholder Action Guide* is a great history and how-to that empowers every investor and comes at a critical time."
—**Rev. Michael H. Crosby, member, Midwest Capuchin Franciscans, and Executive Director, Seventh Generation Interfaith Coalition for Responsible Investment**

D0424321

"Andrew Behar does a masterful job reminding anyone who has investments of our power to influence corporations, which are among the most politically powerful entities on earth today. Citing actual examples of how investors holding a relatively modest amount of stock can push companies to be more sustainable, *The Shareholder Action Guide* provides a wonderful combination of hope for the future and practical advice, in accessible, jargon-free language, on how shareholders can wield their influence. For all who thirst for social and environmental justice, this is an important book to read."

—Kimberly Gluck, Managing Director, Walden Asset Management, and member, Women Donors Network

"*The Shareholder Action Guide* restores the connection between us and our money with practical, achievable steps to push for more accountability and inspiring stories of shareholders who have already made a difference."

—Nell Minow, Vice Chair, ValueEdge Advisors

"Since *Citizens United* gave corporations the rights of citizens, I've wanted to hold them accountable for their bad business practices. *The Shareholder Action Guide* gives everyone a road map on how to do just that."

—Carlynn Rudd, Principal, Caribou Strategies, and Board Member, As You Sow

"As You Sow and Andrew Behar have helped lead the charge for shareholder action in the United States on environmental and societal issues, often ahead of the curve. Here is a unique opportunity to learn from those that actually do."

—Cary Krosinsky, Lecturer, Yale College and Brown University

"We theoretically live in shareholder capitalism. It's shocking, then, how much energy corporate management expends making sure that shareholders' voices are muffled—and how creative, energetic advocacy can remove the gag. Find out how!"

—Carl Pope, Principal, Inside Straight Strategies, and Board Member, As You Sow

"Inspiring stories of successful shareholder advocacy, side-by-side with practical steps for those who want to effect real change through the power of their investments."

—Jennifer McDowell, member, Women Donors Network

"It is exceedingly important to capture history and accounts of how shareholder advocacy has impacted the policies and practices of thousands of companies over the last forty-five years. Behar's book provides an important look at this inspiring history and the differences it helped catalyze."
—**Tim Smith, Director of ESG Shareowner Engagement, Walden Asset Management**

"This book is a must-read for every individual and organization committed to aligning their investments with their mission. Shareholder advocacy is a powerful demonstration of a shared-leadership, shared-responsibility model benefiting everyone from investor to community to the environment. Inspiring!"
—**Lisa Worth Huber, PhD, Chair, Board of Directors, National Peace Academy**

"This book shows how everyday investors can become energized and effective advocates on a range of critical issues facing our planet. Learn directly from pros who share pioneering advocacy wins, part of an important history of change from the community of responsible investors over the last thirty years."
—**Matt Patsky, CEO, Trillium Asset Management**

"This may be the most important book you will ever read if we are going to make the 'Great Transition' from fossil to renewable energy. Behar has given us the framework, architecture, and blueprint on how we get from here to there."
—**Chip Comins, Chairman and CEO, American Renewable Energy Institute**

"*The Shareholder Action Guide* holds the key to empower investors to drive business innovation globally and make the great transition off of fossil fuels to a renewable energy economy. The choice is in our hands as engaged shareholders."
—**Diana Dehm, Host, Sustainability News & Entertainment Radio**

"As shareowners of public companies, we have the right, the responsibility, and the power to help guide companies to be positively impactful. *The Shareholder Action Guide* clearly shows how to be an impact investor in the public markets."
—**Steven J. Schueth, President, First Affirmative Financial Network, and Host/Producer, The SRI Conference**

"Shareholder advocacy is changing the definition of 'business as usual.' Mixing personal stories, strategy, and practical how-tos, *The Shareholder Action Guide* shows how any shareowner can help build a better world."

—Michael Passoff, CEO, Proxy Impact

"For all investors—small and large—who want to make a difference, *The Shareholder Action Guide* offers clear, practical advice. Through shareholder action, investors can urge corporations to change course."

—Kathy Hipple, Corporate Finance Professor, Bard College

"Could the power of ownership change the world? In this excellent primer, Andrew Behar explains how shareholders can hold corporations accountable for their actions and improve both performance and profitability. This is a timely and thoughtful guide to competent and effective activism toward a more durable, resilient, and just society. Behar has written a practical game plan for a world better than that in prospect. The point is that we are not helpless to effect positive change. And that is a powerful message and a clarion call to act."

—David W. Orr, Senior Advisor to the President, Oberlin College

"Through bestowing charitable status, US tax laws enable foundations to leverage social change. Foundations are therefore duty bound to society to use every available tool. This guide provides insights and means essential to foundations to fulfill their social contract."

—John Powers, President, Prentice Foundation

"Shareholder resolutions are an emphatic 'do something' message to corporate leaders from a constituency they can't ignore—the investors who own the company. This excellent guide tells you how to do that."

—Jon M. Jensen, Executive Director, Park Foundation

"The only economy that will allow us to survive the 21st century is one based on ethics, human rights, and sustainability. It will be an economy where people have more rights than corporations and where companies will be accountable to a broader set of stakeholders rather than only shareholders. *The Shareholder Action Guide* is a critical arrow in the quiver to bring this new economy to reality."

—Gary Cohen, President and cofounder, Health Care Without Harm

THE SHAREHOLDER ACTION GUIDE

THE
SHAREHOLDER
ACTION
GUIDE

Unleash Your Hidden Powers to Hold Corporations Accountable

ANDREW BEHAR
CEO of As You Sow

BK

Berrett–Koehler Publishers, Inc.
a BK Currents book

Berrett-Koehler Publishers, Inc.
1333 Broadway, Suite 1000
Oakland, CA 94612-1921
Tel: (510) 817-2277   Fax: (510) 817-2278   www.bkconnection.com

Ordering Information
Quantity sales. Special discounts are available on quantity purchases by corporations, associations, and others. For details, contact the "Special Sales Department" at the Berrett-Koehler address above.
Individual sales. Berrett-Koehler publications are available through most bookstores. They can also be ordered directly from Berrett-Koehler: Tel: (800) 929-2929; Fax: (802) 864-7626; www.bkconnection.com
Orders for college textbook/course adoption use. Please contact Berrett-Koehler: Tel: (800) 929-2929; Fax: (802) 864-7626.
Orders by U.S. trade bookstores and wholesalers. Please contact Ingram Publisher Services, Tel: (800) 509-4887; Fax: (800) 838-1149; E-mail: customer.service@ingrampublisherservices.com; or visit www.ingrampublisherservices.com/Ordering for details about electronic ordering.

Berrett-Koehler and the BK logo are registered trademarks of Berrett-Koehler Publishers, Inc.

Printed in the United States of America

Berrett-Koehler books are printed on long-lasting acid-free paper. When it is available, we choose paper that has been manufactured by environmentally responsible processes. These may include using trees grown in sustainable forests, incorporating recycled paper, minimizing chlorine in bleaching, or recycling the energy produced at the paper mill.

Library of Congress Cataloging-in-Publication Data

Names: Behar, Andrew, 1957-
Title: The shareholder action guide : unleash your hidden powers to hold
    corporations accountable / by Andrew Behar ; edited by Conrad
MacKerron.
Description: First Edition. | Oakland, CA : Berrett-Koehler Publishers,
2016.
    | Includes bibliographical references and index.
Identifiers: LCCN 2016025596 | ISBN 9781626568457 (pbk.)
Subjects: LCSH: Stockholders' meetings. | Corporate meetings. | Corporate
    culture.
Classification: LCC HD2743.5 .B44 2016 | DDC 338.7--dc23
LC record available at https://lccn.loc.gov/2016025596

Cover Design: Susan Malikowski/DesignLeaf Studio

Cover Image: VasjaKomen

Author Image: Sarah Sackner

Book Production: Adept Content Solutions

Figure 1, opposite page: *Used with permission Tom Toro / The New Yorker Collection / www.cartoonbank.com.*

"Yes, the planet got destroyed, but for a beautiful moment in time we created a lot of value for shareholders."

CONTENTS

CHAPTER 12 **How Do I Know What I Own?**   **127**

It is nearly impossible to know what stocks are embedded in your funds, but there are new tools to help you.

CHAPTER 13 **How to Get Your Company to Offer Funds Aligned with Your Values**   **133**

Talk to your colleagues, contact your plan administrator, and bring a solution to the table. There are specific processes to go through.

CHAPTER 14 **A New Generation of Corporate Leaders**   **139**

Some CEOs have changed their corporate cultures to embrace environmental, social, and governance issues and they are outperforming those who do not—why?

CHAPTER 15 **Time to Take Back Your Power**   **143**

Shareholder advocates are the leading force in bringing important transformations into practice for a just, safe, and clean future.

RESOURCE A Acknowledgments and Biographies of Interviewed Leaders   **145**

RESOURCE B Links   **151**

Proxy Voting Guidelines, Proxy Preview®, and others

RESOURCE C Alliance Building for a Shareholder Movement   **153**

RESOURCE D Glossary and Acronyms   **157**

FOREWORD

by Thomas Van Dyck,
As You Sow Founder and Board Chair

In 1992, I founded the As You Sow Foundation based on the Biblical reference that a person reaps what they sow. The original mission was to hold corporations accountable for compliance with a unique California law (Proposition 65) requiring warning labels on products with toxic or carcinogenic ingredients. We donated the winnings from these lawsuits to fund grassroots activist groups. In 1997, after struggling with various ways to make shareholder advocacy more effective inside of a financial services institution, I decided there could be numerous benefits to doing it in a nonprofit setting and created a second program at As You Sow, the Corporate Social Responsibility Program, to pursue shareholder advocacy.

Pressing companies as investors in a nonprofit setting allowed my team to work with a wide range of stakeholders. With the leadership of Program Director Conrad MacKerron and Associate Director Michael Passoff, we brought new sophistication to Environment Social and Governance (ESG)–issue shareholder advocacy, doing extensive research into the economic impacts of target issues to develop a business case for investors in promoting proposals. We developed an active "get out the vote" solicitation campaign that was uncommon for ESG proposals.

We were joined by visionary foundation leaders and their brilliant boards: Tim Smith and the amazing religious orders of Interfaith Center for Corporate Responsibility, John Powers and The Educational Foundation of America, Adelaide Gomer and the Park Foundation, and Ellen Dorsey and the Wallace Global Foundation, who were all early adopters of having 100 percent of their money in alignment with their values.

We have partnered with leading groups including Divest-Invest Philanthropy, Rainforest Action Network, Greenpeace, Headwaters Forest Coalition, and Ruckus Society to work on issues around saving old-growth forests, recycling electronic waste, and creating codes of conduct to stop the use of sweat-shops combining campaigning, organizing, and investing to create a powerful nexus pushing for change.

As You Sow's Corporate Social Responsibility Program, which started out as an experiment 20 years ago, has developed into a widely respected player in the shareholder advocacy community. I am excited and proud of what we have accomplished, featuring a staff of incredible leaders: Conrad MacKerron, Danielle Fugere, and Patricia Jurewicz. Thank you all for your brilliance and your tireless commitment to speak truth to power.

In the *Shareholder Action Guide*, Andrew Behar tells inspiring stories of leaders from the sustainable investment, religious and labor communities who have skillfully utilized their power as investors to stand up to corporations to improve how they treat people and the planet. Wherever we have had a victory, we have never been alone. Always, the work of a multitude of organiza-tions and strategies has made the shift. The inspiring campaigns profiled in these pages have helped to advance shareholder advo-cacy to the point where it is a highly effective strategy to comple-ment legislation, litigation, and grassroots activism as a key tool for social change. We have been honored to be on this journey with so many leaders. I hope you'll join the movement.

INTRODUCTION

You Have More Power Than You Think

The world is out of balance. Modern society is faced with enormous challenges—the highest levels of income disparity in modern times; abusive labor conditions; toxins in our water supply; pollution of air, sea, and land; climate change threatening our future; and rampant corruption. The big question is, who's in control?

The answer is corporations. Taken in aggregate, corporate power is greater than that of governments, religions, and civil society. Corporations are the most powerful entities on the planet, and in the United States they now have rights as "people" to make unlimited political contributions to gain even more influence.

Yet, these same publicly traded corporations are, by design, beholden to their shareholders, people like you and me. We have the power to change these companies. We are the owners. In fact an estimated 48 percent of adult Americans[1] or approximately 91 million people have some ownership stake in public companies either as part of a fund or in individual stocks.

However, the vast majority of us abdicate our power or are simply not aware that we possess it in the first place.

While you may believe that there is nothing that you can do, the exact opposite is true. One individual can make enormous change. And by teaming up with other like-minded investors, you can magnify your impact. You have rights and much more

1

influence than you think to help the corporations that you have ownership in become responsible to their employees, customers, communities, and the planet. By doing so, they can also become more profitable.

As an owner of even one share of stock, you have the right to vote on critical issues, elect the board of directors, and weigh in on CEO pay at nearly every annual meeting through your proxy, which is the company's ballot of issues for shareholders to vote on.

You can take direct action by engaging corporate managers and executives. If it's a US company and you own as little as $2,000 in stock for one year, you can file a shareholder resolution asking for disclosure or a shift in corporate behavior on environmental, social, and governance policies.

As the owner of shares in mutual funds or exchange-traded funds or a contributor to a pension fund, you have rights to lobby your fund managers to demand that they vote and engage the companies that they own on your behalf.

At many companies, if you are part of a coalition of investors owning three percent of the stock for three years, you recently gained the right to nominate a board candidate of your choosing that the company must place on the annual proxy for a shareholder vote.

If change is not happening fast enough or in a credible way, you can make a powerful public statement by divesting your holdings. This sends the message that these companies are not acting in the best interest of long term shareholders, are creating significant financial risk, or are causing unacceptable harm to people or the environment.

You may have heard the term *shareholder activism* before. It can refer to at least two kinds of corporate engagement, with very different motivations and outcomes. Often shareholder activism refers to a major shareholder or group of shareholders seeking to use its influence solely for its own economic gain by using the proxy process to change management or board members, or for a hostile takeover of a company. Examples of this kind of shareholder campaign include AOL's takeover of Time Warner or Carl Icahn's attempt to take over Clorox.[2] That's not what this book is about.

We prefer to call the process of positive engagement on environmental, social, and governance (ESG) issues *shareholder advocacy*. The intent is to use the power of share ownership to improve the company's reputation and long-term financial success by enhancing ESG practices and policies. These actions are seen as a collaboration with the company, not an intent to intimidate or take over the company. To make things a bit more complicated, though, it's also true that some of the governance or G in ESG can focus more on economic than social performance, as when a large pension fund seeks votes on CEO pay or to try to replace an underperforming board member. Both activism and advocacy can overlap in the use of a tactic, but the intent and outcome are very different.

The *Shareholder Action Guide* offers practical ways to help you unleash your hidden powers to hold publicly traded corporations accountable. Shareholder advocates interviewed in these pages have forced the tobacco giant RJR to cease marketing Camel cigarettes to children, been instrumental in halting the clear-cutting of old-growth forests, worked to end abusive labor practices, pushed fracking companies to disclose the harmful environmental impact of their practices, and gotten rid of under-qualified corporate board members, to name just a few of their accomplishments.

This book provides the tools and knowledge to become an empowered shareholder and push for these kinds of changes yourself. It instructs how to enlist allies and advocates to fight for the changes you desire and how to use new tools to assist you as you peer through the veils of obfuscation that mask corporate policies and action.

The challenge is great; US-based corporations comprising the Fortune 500 earn tens of trillions in gross revenues each year. In the United States, there are about 3,700 companies actively traded on the New York Stock Exchange and NASDAQ.[3] Along with all that money comes tremendous political power.

Shareholders not only have strength in numbers, but the legal right and the moral obligation to exert their influence. We have had this right since the 1930s and used it successfully thousands of times. Today we have resources at our fingertips that, even a few years ago, were available only to elite financial managers. The online research tools detailed in this book give us the ability to know what holdings are embedded in our retirement funds and learn about corporate assets, officers, and their actions (and inactions) with unprecedented ease. Social media platforms give us the ability to communicate instantly on a global scale at virtually no cost. Together, these tools give us the power to band together as never before and bring about positive and lasting change.

We have entered an era in which shareholders can and must shoulder their responsibility and unleash their power. This is no time to sit back helplessly and say, "But there is nothing I can do." Now is the time to join the global movement of shareholder advocates and take action to shape the world into the just and sustainable future that we desire.

1

Who Let the Dog Out?

If your dog escaped from your yard and rampaged around the neighborhood, knocking garbage cans into the street, your neighbor would probably show up at your door, and you would, of course, accept responsibility and clean up the mess, scold your dog, and fix the fence.

OWNERSHIP IMPLIES RESPONSIBILITY

What about your investments? Perhaps, like 91 million Americans, you own stocks directly in companies or funds that are composed of dozens, hundreds, or even thousands of stocks. Are you responsible for the behavior of these companies?

If a company that you own causes an oil spill that does damage (like your dog did in the neighborhood), would you feel that this is your responsibility? Or would you think,

Figure 2: Are you responsible for your dog's actions? *Photo used with permission of the author.*

"That's for management and the board to deal with." Do you give it a second thought? Do you even track the activities of the companies that you own?

Although the corporation shields investors from direct legal liability, moral responsibility is another story: Do you want a company that you've invested in—and that is benefitting you financially—to act in ways that are contrary to your values? In addition, can you use your influence as a shareowner to help your company become more profitable and have a positive impact on society by adopting policies that enhance its image, increase employee retention, and reduce risk from liability?

> Supreme Court Justice Louis Brandeis stated the matter succinctly, "There is no such thing to my mind . . . as an innocent stockholder. He may be innocent in fact, but socially he cannot be held innocent. He accepts the benefits of the system. It is his business and his obligation to see that those who represent him carry out a policy which is consistent with public welfare."[4]

THEORY OF CHANGE

For our society to be sustainable—that is, to provide sustenance and continuity for all people and ecosystems for generations to come—we must first acknowledge that today we are out of balance and need to find a way to change.

Over the past century corporate power has become the most dominant force on the planet. Of the 150 largest economic entities in the world, 87 are corporations—that's 58 percent.[5] This concentration of resources gives corporations power and influence over their employees, communities, and the governments in which they operate. This lopsided power relationship means that corporations can disregard the impact that their activities have on the rest of society. They can commit human rights abuses and choose to pollute low-income and minority communities near their plants. They can manipulate political power to their financial advantage. They can choose to ignore dire warnings of global catastrophe caused by their activities. If local governments intervene, the corporation can shift their activities to the other side of the globe or alter the government.

According to US Senator Elizabeth Warren (D-Mass.),

> **Corporate criminals routinely escape meaningful prosecution for their misconduct. In a single year, in case after case, across many sectors of the economy, federal agencies caught big companies breaking the law—defrauding taxpayers, covering up deadly safety problems, even precipitating the financial collapse in 2008—and let them off the hook with barely a slap on the wrist. Often, companies paid meager fines, which some will try to write off as a tax deduction.**[6]

What the executives who head corporations cannot do is ignore the people who own their companies. They work for the shareholders. While shareholders indeed have enormous power, most still care primarily about maximizing profit. However, a growing number are choosing to leverage their power to improve the environmental, social, and governance ESG practices of the public companies they hold for the dual purpose of maintaining long-term profitability and positively impacting society and the planet. Once motivated, shareholders can become the single most powerful force for creating positive, lasting change in corporate behavior.

It is critical for corporate leaders to address the impact of their policies and actions. By ignoring this impact they are creating risk for their customers, employees, shareholders, and themselves. Ultimately, companies that measure their success not just in terms of the next quarterly statement, but in years and decades, will be better able to evaluate and reduce their long-term risk. Shareholders have a responsibility to work with corporations to undertake this broader risk analysis, make this information available, and make sure that decisions are made that benefit their own long-term profitability as well as humanity and the planet.

A LOT OF McCUPS

To use a concrete example, let's say that it's early 2011 and you own $2,000 worth of McDonald's stock. Every morning before work, you go through the drive-in and get an Egg McMuffin, hash browns, and a McCafe caramel mocha latte.

At work, you finish your coffee and, since the polystyrene foam cup is not recyclable, toss it in the garbage can—its first stop on the way to the landfill. You recall that McDonald's got rid of the foam clamshell years ago—in 1990,[7] in fact—and wonder why they're still using cups made of the same material. Foam keeps the coffee warm, and it's probably cheap to manufacture, but isn't foam made of polystyrene, a petroleum-based plastic? Doesn't it last forever, just crumbling into smaller and smaller bits that are ingested by birds and fish? Hasn't the styrene used to make the cups been cited as a possible carcinogen?

The next morning at McD's you ask if they have any other types of cups—maybe one that doesn't break down into harmful particles of resin and can be more easily recycled? They tell you no, that's it.

Later that day, you do a little research and learn that for their 68 million daily customers, McDonald's is using foam cups at 35,000 restaurants in 118 countries! You also see that they have no recycling program (other than for cooking oil), and you do the math.[8] It comes to about 770 million foam cups per year in the United States.

The next day, rather than go through the drive-through window, you go into the restaurant and ask some of the other customers if they think it would be a good idea for McDonald's to switch to a more environmentally friendly coffee cup. Several of them like the idea. You bring this information to the manager, who says she'd like to switch, but it's a franchise, and she must buy her supplies from McDonald's. What power does she have?

You leave discouraged. As you drive to the office, it seems like every other person on the road is sipping from a foam cup. Throughout the day, you can't stop thinking about those billions of cups strewn across the beaches of the world. You calculate that the

Great Pacific Garbage Patch, which consists of small bits of plastic suspended throughout the water column[9] now estimated to be twice the size of Texas, just keeps getting bigger. Finally, you had heard that the World Economic Forum predicted that there will be more plastic than fish, by weight, in the world's oceans by 2050![10]

The following morning you wake up with a brilliant idea: maybe you can get all of the owners of McDonald's stock, like you, to vote on the idea of switching to a greener coffee cup. Like you, the other shareholders probably believe McDonald's is a company destined to grow over the years. All those cups going to the landfills bother you and present a risk to the company. Also, as a shareholder, you feel it's bad for the company brand to be associated with this toxic mess, because if people knew what was happening, that could drive the value of your shares down. Using foam cups when something better is available also shows that management is not thinking about the big picture, and you can't help wondering what else they're not considering.

But almost as soon as the idea to ask the company to use a more environmentally friendly cup occurs to you, you dismiss it. How would you get in touch with all the owners of the stock? And who would listen to your proposal, anyway? After all, you own just $2,000 worth of stock, and the company is worth more than $115 billion.[11]

The fact is, you're in luck. As the owner of even $2,000 worth of stock that you have held for a year, you have the right to submit a shareholder resolution, which by law, if properly written, the corporation is obligated to put to a vote of all of its shareholders on the company's shareholder proxy or ballot at their annual meeting.

This is exactly what happened in 2011 at As You Sow, the nonprofit organization that I lead.

After a dialogue asking McDonald's to fix the problem went nowhere, we filed a shareholder resolution, asking the company to replace polystyrene cups with more environmentally beneficial ones. Our mission is to increase environmental and social corporate responsibility and engage companies on critical issues. These engagements often lead to filing a shareholder resolution, one of the strategies we employ to motivate corporations to act more responsibly.

Led by our Senior Vice President, Conrad MacKerron, who specializes in issues of sustainability and waste, we felt that Mc-Donald's needed just such a push. The company had switched away from polystyrene clamshells in 1990,[12] so they clearly understood how switching to a less harmful cup could improve their sustainability and enhance their brand.

McDonald's had never faced a shareholder resolution about this issue, and that was the game changer. The resolution came up for a vote and was approved by 29 percent of the shareholders.

Voting on shareholder resolutions is different than a standard political vote. If you were running for mayor and got only 29 percent of the vote, you'd likely consider it a failure. But think how a publically traded company would react to a hedge fund or a single shareholder who owned 29 percent of its stock. Such a person would likely be on their board and have enormous clout. Also the vote was a nonbinding recommendation to the company. The fact that a large minority of its shareholders voted in favor of moving away from harmful materials and avoiding the risks associated with it sent an important message to the company.

The vote brought McDonald's management to the table for discussions, yet over the course of a year, they still had not taken any real action, so the resolution was filed again. This time, however, the shareholder action got more attention because of a successful campaign in California led by Clean Water Action, the SurfRider Foundation,[13] and other local groups. The effort cosponsored groundbreaking legislation and helped support grassroots leaders to pass 65 local ordinances to ban polystyrene in restaurants.[14] The California effort gained significant national press attention, and combined with shareholder pressure, was enough that McDonald's agreed to a pilot program, swapping out foam for recyclable cups in 2,000 West coast locations. In exchange the resolution was withdrawn because the company "indicated its intent to take several positive, substantive steps in response to our concerns about use of polystyrene foam-based beverage cups and lack of a comprehensive recycling policy for on-site beverage and food containers."

The pilot was a huge success with customers and in the press. A year later the program was rolled out to all 14,000 US stores. It also set a goal to reduce food and packaging waste by 50 percent in several top markets by 2020 that will require increased recycling efforts. McDonald's periodically reports the results of its ongoing efforts to reduce packaging waste and the deployment of more environmentally responsible materials. It has a significant incentive to expand and improve its packaging stewardship programs, actions that are perceived positively by both shareholders and the public. Additionally, the positive brand image has huge value for the company—a win for McDonald's, its shareholders, and the planet.

This is just one example of how active shareholders can step forward to present an opportunity for a company to shift a policy or adopt a better business plan and then lead an industry. Often it is a shift that management may not be considering but that will ultimately benefit the company in many ways. At the same time, shareholders, employees, and other stakeholders enjoy increased share value, and the environment gets a break, too.

THE POWER OF THE PROXY

You may be a novice investor, or you may be vastly experienced, but in all probability you aren't really aware of the power you have as a shareholder. I wasn't aware myself until I was introduced to my current job. Shareholders can have significant impact on the behavior of huge corporations on issues as diverse as human rights, diversity in the workplace and the board, carbon emissions, and much more. Shareholders have the right to engage corporate management—sometimes escalating to the filing of shareholder resolutions, which is one of the many tools available to investors who wish to promote more environmentally and socially responsible behavior on the part of companies in which they invest.

DOES ENGAGEMENT HARM CORPORATE PERFORMANCE?

There are simple ways that every investor can directly impact and shape their investments to align with their values. You may be surprised to learn that the corporations that are more responsive to their shareholders and enact more positive ESG policies have improved performance. In fact, according to a Deutsche Bank Group report[15] that looked at "more than 100 academic studies of sustainable investing around the world and then closely examined and categorized 56 research papers as well as two literature reviews and four meta studies," the often-held assumption that sustainable investing yields "mixed results" is not accurate. In fact, the report shows that "Corporate Social Responsibility and most importantly, Environmental, Social, and Governance" (ESG) factors are correlated with superior risk-adjusted returns." Furthermore, they state that 89 percent of the studies show that companies with high ESG ratings exhibit market outperformance and that "SRI fund returns show neutral or mixed results."

This finding is backed up by research from TIAA-CREF[16] that reports, "A TIAA-CREF analysis of leading SRI equity indexes over the long-term found no statistical difference in returns compared to broad market benchmarks, suggesting the absence of any systematic performance penalty."

In addition, the California Public Employee Retirement System (CalPERS), the largest pension fund in the United States, has found that when it engages with companies in its portfolio, it sees increased returns. "Approximately 188 companies selected by the Pension Fund publicly and privately since 1987 on average outperformed the Russell 1000 by 14.4 percent over the five years after CalPERS began engagement, commonly referred to as the "CalPERS Effect." The companies lagged the index by nearly 39 percent in the three years prior to CalPERS involvement.[17]

Finally, a June 2015 survey by the Certified Financial Analyst Institute[18] (CFA) indicated that 73 percent of portfolio managers and research analysts take ESG issues into account in making

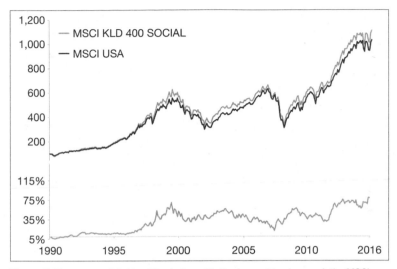

Figure 3: The responsible investing index with the longest track record, the MSCI KLD 400 Social index,[19] started in 1990 as the Domini 400 Social Index. It is one of the first SRI indexes and has outperformed the S&P 500 index since its inception. If you had invested $1 million in 1990, you would have made $10 million in the S&P and $11 million in the MSCI KLD 400. *Source: MSCI. Reprinted with permission. MSCI retains all other rights, title, and interest in and to the work.*

investment decisions, with governance being the most common concern.

This should not be a surprise. Companies that are less engaged with their shareholders are less open to new ideas and may not perceive risks. After all, a better management team—more aware of the impacts of corporate policy—will make better decisions and long-term investments to optimize efficiency and reduce risk. These attitudes at the board and management levels translate into long-term sustainable growth and become woven into the DNA of the corporation.

DISCREDIT WHERE DISCREDIT IS DUE

In 1970, economist Milton Friedman's essay, "The Social Responsibility of Business Is to Increase Its Profits" argued that business basically had no responsibility other than to maximize profits for shareholders. However, the demonstrated success of socially screened investing and the emergence of corporate social responsibility initiatives have discredited Friedman's view.

Now, many Fortune 500 executives enthusiastically endorse the notion of corporate social responsibility (CSR) as part of a company's obligation to all stakeholders, including customers, employees, investors, and advocates, as well as something that pays its way. All of these activities can be evaluated by performance indicators, including reduced operating costs, enhanced brand image, increased sales and productivity, employee retention, and reduced regulatory costs and oversight. Some of the strategies and practices include:

- A commitment to diversity in hiring employees and barring discrimination

- Treating employees as assets rather than costs[20]

- Creating high performance workplaces that integrate the views of line employees into the decision-making processes

- Adoption of performance goals that go beyond compliance with environmental rules to promote measures to reduce ecological footprints, such as the United Nations Principles for Responsible Investment (UNPRI[21]) and the CERES Principles[22]

- Advanced resource productivity, focused on the use of natural resources in a more productive, efficient, and profitable fashion like maximizing recycled content and product and packaging recycling

- Responsibility for the conditions under which goods are produced down the entire supply chain and by contract employees domestically or abroad

- Transparent reporting on greenhouse gas emission, water use, and carbon footprint

INVESTOR CLOUT

The power to effect these meaningful changes in corporate behavior starts with voting your proxies, which a majority of shareowners either don't do or leave to proxy voting services. If they do not vote, their votes are given to management. It's as though investors are citizens and aren't aware that they have the right to go to the ballot box to choose their elected officials.

However, through voting proxies, engaging with corporations, and initiating proxy votes about critical issues, investors can—and have—significantly influenced corporate behavior on issues ranging from lesbian, gay, bisexual, and transgender (LGBT) rights, board diversity, fair labor, and protecting the environment to corporate governance, hiring practices, animal rights, and many other issues.

The truth is, the dog slipped under the fence a long time ago. It's time to bring it to heel.

2

How Ordinary Investors Can Bring Real Change to Big Problems

Have you ever called a major corporation to correct a problem? Once you've navigated the endless phone tree and listened to a symphony's worth of scratchy hold music, you're finally connected to a representative who, with studied empathy, asks how she can help. This alone feels like a victory. With luck, they'll correct the problem, and, although there are periods of aggravation during your quest, you hang up, satisfied. As far as it goes, the system works.

However, exactly who do you email about slave labor used in the manufacture of your cell phone? Who do you call if you're distressed because your donut contains nanoparticles that are small enough to penetrate the blood-brain barrier? How do you find out if your hamburger comes from a steer raised on a concentrated feedlot where it is fed antibiotics? What's Big Agriculture's 800 number so you can ask farmers to stop using genetically modified organisms (GMOs)? How do you air your concerns about excessive CEO pay, lack of diversity in the workplace, packaging that is destroying the ocean ecosystems, toxic dumping on the poorest minority groups, the risks of fracking, or the decimation of the rainforests?

Many companies' operational details and supply chain, if publicly known, would change the way their customers view their brands. Advocates are not creating the risky behavior; the corporations are doing this themselves through lax policies and short-term thinking. Advocates bring the information to the public's attention through a variety of means. If this results in customers deciding to buy products from a company with mindful policies over one that appears to not care, then let the market decide.

A NEW ERA IN SHAREHOLDER ADVOCACY

Now imagine that your concern is something as huge as systematic racial discrimination that isn't even in the United States but 6,000 miles away in South Africa, and it's 1971, before the advent of the Internet, let alone social media. The system you oppose is called *apartheid*, and it is as entrenched in South Africa as the greed and racism of those who instituted it when they colonized this region of the world. What can you do?

This was the situation when attorney Paul Neuhauser and the Episcopal Society for Cultural Racial Unity (ESCRU) decided they had to take action. The South African government had already ignored stiff sanctions and embargoes imposed by the United Nations. Protests around the world were beginning to coalesce into what would become a powerful global divestment movement. However, Neuhauser believed he could do something to force rapid change.

ESCRU's mission was to fight segregation in the United States. Neuhauser focused on the apartheid problem because it was his goal to bring the organization's investment portfolio into line with its mission—and Neuhauser had a novel way to do it. ESCRU owned shares in General Motors, which was the largest employer of blacks in South Africa. Neuhauser believed that by operating in South Africa, GM was tacitly endorsing apartheid. Of course, ESCRU could have simply sold the shares it owned and thereby distanced itself from GM's practices. But selling those shares would have had little impact on the corporation, which was, after all, the largest car manufacturer in the world, with operations on every continent except Antarctica.

Despite ESCRU's relatively small ownership stake, Neuhauser realized he could use it as leverage to compel GM to change. On behalf of ESCRU he filed a shareholder resolution, asking GM to end discriminatory practices at its South African operations.

Shareholder resolutions have been allowed by the Securities and Exchange Commission since the 1930s, but until Neuhauser's filing, they had, for the most part, been employed by large investors in arcane matters of corporate governance. By filing a shareholder resolution pertaining to a social concern, Neuhauser was perhaps the first of what have come to be known as shareholder advocates.

FUROR IN THE BOARDROOM

Pioneering actions are not always celebrated, and that was especially true in the case of ESCRU's shareholder resolution, which caused a furor in the GM boardroom. Many contentious negotiations proceeded from there, as GM begged for the resolution to be withdrawn. But Neuhauser and ESCRU stood firm.

Ultimately, the company adopted what were known as the Sullivan Principles,[23] created by Reverend Leon Sullivan, a Baptist minister, civil rights leader, and social advocate who was the first African American on GM's board. The Sullivan Principles were workplace rules that specified policies such as equal pay for equal work, increasing the number of blacks and nonwhites in management and supervisory positions, and the elimination of discriminatory workplace practices such as segregation of restrooms, eating areas, and drinking fountains. If these actions did not bring about the end of apartheid in ten years, Sullivan called for all companies doing business in South Africa to divest their operations in the country. These principles became a blueprint for ending apartheid.

FOLLOW THE LEADER

Then, perhaps feeling shamed by comparison with GM's actions, other large American corporations doing business in South

Africa, including Goodyear and Ford, also adopted the Sullivan Principles. Although neither GM nor the other companies ceased operations in South Africa, the changes they made struck a major blow against apartheid because within South Africa, there was now an example of a nonsegregated workplace. The modern era of shareholder advocacy was born, and in concert with global social protests, the growing divestment movement, and the courage of the South African people, change would come. Most often, lasting impact is accomplished through the coordination of shareholder advocacy and ongoing social efforts. The two work together—two tools in the social change tool box.

That was decades ago, but the impact of this shareholder resolution can still be felt. Since 1971, the scope of issues that have been addressed by shareholder resolutions—broadly falling under the umbrella of environmental, social, and governance (ESG) issues—has greatly expanded. Shareholder advocates have successfully brought about changes in a vast number of industries.

We'll get into all of the details of how to file a shareholder resolution later on, but for now, it's important to know that resolutions are, in general, nonbinding, or, to use the legal term, *precatory*, which is a request to a corporation's board of directors to take certain action.

At first glance, it may seem that a request like this wouldn't carry much weight with a corporate board. However, as Neuhauser's resolution with GM showed, that request can challenge a board with a compelling moral or financial choice. When thoughtful people come together to identify and address a problem, solutions are often found. This is the essence of why shareholder advocates work to enlist the corporations that are often most responsible for the problem.

Though paraphrased and grossly simplified, some examples of shareholder resolutions could be boiled down to requests such as:

- Please write a report showing the potential negative impact to our corporate brand to be associated with using slave labor in the manufacture of our products.

- Please tell all shareholders how our company's capital is being spent on political lobbying and how this may create potential brand risk.

- Please write a report showing how it would reduce potential shareholder risk if our company took action to stop the dumping of thousands of tons of electronic waste into landfills.

- Please identify better ways to source our products than destroying the rainforests for lumber and paper, and quantify how making this change will increase our brand reputation and, therefore, our competiveness.

- Please explain to shareholders why we are spending billions of dollars exploring and drilling for oil when the reserves already on our balance sheet will most likely be stranded, and this activity contributes to climate change.

Questions like these are drafted into 500-word shareholder resolutions and presented to all investors in a company for a vote at the annual meeting. They can become the hot topic of debate in the media. Customers and employees soon associate the brand with the issue. You can see that management and the board are under enormous pressure to respond and take action. That is the power that you have as a shareholder to bring these ideas forth and hold corporations accountable.

3

What You Can Ask a Corporation to Do

In 1971, the British blues-rock band Ten Years After had a Top-40 hit with the lyrics "I'd love to change the world / But I don't know what to do / So I'll leave it up to you."

The song may reflect the frustration and confusion of the time. Ironically, perhaps, it also surrenders to confusion and leaves it up to others to take action.

Fortunately, hundreds of thousands of people have chosen to not leave the work up to others and have taken action themselves. Whether you are voting your proxies, contacting legislators, calling and writing to corporate leaders, signing petitions, participating in demonstrations, boycotting certain products or companies, filing or co-filing a resolution, or divesting, your participation in bringing about positive reforms has an impact around the world and across the global economy.

CIVIL SOCIETY COMING TOGETHER

As Mahatma Gandhi said, "When the people lead, the leaders will follow."[24] Contrary to popular belief, policy makers in general follow civil society. Our "leaders" are actually our followers, and there are many ways for each of us to lead, but it takes coordination and strategy to build a movement.

An example of a global problem that brought people together to analyze and solve it occurred when in May of 1985 scientists discovered a hole in the ozone layer caused by human-made chlorofluorocarbons (CFCs). Global leaders rapidly came together, and by September 1987 (yes, just 28 months later) The Montreal Protocol on Substances That Deplete the Ozone Layer[25] was ratified. Today, according to *National Geographic*, the problem appears to be abated, as it reported, "What would the 1980s have been without 'big hair' and ice-cold wine coolers? Luckily no one had to find out. Key substitutions in hairsprays and refrigerants allowed such products to exist without CFCs, which were found to be ripping a huge 'hole' in Earth's protective ozone layer."[26]

Corporate action to stop a solution can also happen. Climate change was also identified as a global risk by scientists in the mid-1970s. It has taken the world four decades to come to agreement that there is a problem and develop a plan for action. This is a testament to the power and influence of corporations to stop progress. Many resources were spent to create scientific confusion and block a solution.

The good news is that students, the faith-based community (including the pope, the World Council of Churches, and a conference of Muslim Mullahs[27]), policy makers, litigators, a broad civil society movement, and shareholders have come together to address this global problem. Like South African divestment, there is a huge moral contradiction for shareholders who own companies that continue to dump carbon pollution into the atmosphere, destroying humanity's shared commons. The difference is that these companies also have unprecedented financial risk. The moral issue plus the fiduciary risk has pushed this issue to the forefront of today's global consciousness, and there is now a coordinated global movement to demand action.

ENVIRONMENTAL, SOCIAL, AND GOVERNANCE POLICIES

By asking for action on ESG policies, a lot can be accomplished by active, thoughtful shareholders. But there are rules and limitations—micro-management is not allowed. Asking Chevron to change the colors of its logo, suggesting that Burger King introduce hot-fudge French fries, or petitioning Google to delete some embarrassing images may be omitted by the company from the proxy statement as the Securities and Exchange Commission (SEC) would probably construe those things as "ordinary business"—how a company runs its business on a daily basis. These are not allowed in a shareholder resolution, but we'll take a deeper look into the nuances of SEC rules later.

For now, let's look at the broad areas in which shareholders do have considerable influence with corporations. Whether you are working independently or with an advocacy nonprofit organization, a faith-based institution, a pension fund, or a socially responsible asset manager, these issues pertain to a corporation's ESG policies. In the broadest sense, here's what those words mean in the context of shareholder advocacy.

Environmental: Nearly all corporations have an impact on the environment. If they manufacture or sell products, their operations affect the environment at some point in their production, transportation, or supply chain. The way a given corporation handles supply-chain issues under the umbrella of the environment is of concern to investors because the company may be, for example, using environmentally damaging mining, farming, or logging operations, thus creating risk and liability, which would affect shareholder value. The company has choices to make, and if its policies are clear and it considers looking at the larger system in which it operates, it can create great products with far less impact. These are some examples of environmental issues:

- Energy use and its impact on climate change
- Hydraulic fracturing (impact on water and air)
- Methane emissions and flaring
- Air pollution
- Water pollution
- Waste disposal and incineration
- Recycling

- Food toxicity
- Chemicals in consumer products
- Pesticides and herbicides

Social: By being in business and hiring people to work either directly or through suppliers, corporations intrinsically have a social impact, and investors have a legitimate concern about this impact. If, for example, a corporation's hiring practices are discriminatory, they do not pay a living wage, and abuses or physical risks exist at company facilities, the corporation is exposing itself to potential liability, litigation, or regulation. If a corporation or its suppliers use abusive labor practices in their operations, here or abroad, this can harm the brand's reputation and standing in the community and therefore its value. These are some examples of social issues:

- Human rights
- Indigenous rights
- Human trafficking
- Slave labor
- Fair pay
- Political spending
- Workplace diversity
- Decent work
- Conflict zone operations
- Tobacco
- Prison and executions
- Guns
- Data privacy

Governance: Publicly traded corporations have a board of directors and various executives who direct and manage the operation of the company. If board members or executives are underqualified, not diverse, overcompensated, have conflicts of interest, or are neglecting their fiduciary duties, investor value may be harmed, and the company may create legal liabilities. These are some governance issues:

- Executive compensation (CEO pay)
- Reporting and transparency
- Business ethics
- Board diversity
- Board oversight
- CEO / board chair split
- Shareholder right to nominate board candidates
- Stock buybacks
- Political spending and lobbying
- Unlimited and untraceable "dark money" given by corporations to influence elections

CAN'T I JUST STATE MY CASE TO THE BOARD OF DIRECTORS?

In short, yes. One way to make a statement is to vote your proxy. Another is to file or co-file a shareholder resolution. You can also attend the annual general meeting (AGM) where you may get a few minutes at the microphone. These few moments, in which you are speaking directly to management and the company's board of directors, can be used to raise key—and sometimes unforgettable—points.

One memorable and dramatic statement occurred in 1992 at the AGM of Time Warner Corporation. There, the late actor Charlton Heston—a minor shareholder—took his turn at the open microphone, and before the assembled executives and shareholders, he read aloud the lyrics to the song "Cop Killer," released on a Time Warner record label.

The song had already ignited robust social controversy, with critics including President George W. Bush, Tipper Gore, and police organizations across the country citing concerns that it promoted violence against police. The song's writer, rapper Ice-T, defended the song as an anthem of protest against police brutality and denied that it posed any risk to law enforcement.

It must be remembered that Heston portrayed Moses in Cecil B. DeMille's 1956 blockbuster *The Ten Commandments*, and in one memorable scene he parted the Red Sea. Though not quite as dramatic, his performance before Time Warner shareholders generated its own divide—a cultural one about violence in the media. Gun rights advocates took one side. Civil libertarians squared off against them. The ultimate result wasn't any dramatic change in Time Warner's corporate culture, but it did bring into focus a significant social conflict that the company's product had created.

In a more recent example, at the Walt Disney Company's AGM in March 2015, Dr. Stan Glantz,[28] the American Legacy Foundation Distinguished Professor of Tobacco Control at the University of California San Francisco, and Gina Intinarelli,[29] Executive Director, Office of Population Health and Accountable Care at UCSF and a registered nurse, took the podium during a period allocated for public comment and delivered impassioned statements about the public health crisis that portraying images of smoking in youth-rated movies is causing, implicating all Hollywood studios.

They cited, among other evidence, published reports from the US Surgeon General and the Centers for Disease Control (CDC) that showed how Hollywood's portrayal of smoking leads children to take up the habit and begin a life-long addiction, and that an R rating for all movies containing smoking imagery could save 1,000,000 lives.[30, 31]

Disney CEO and Board Chair Bob Iger was so moved by their comments that he announced from the podium that Disney would put an "ironclad policy in place" to remove all smoking for any films rated G, PG, or PG-13 that Disney produces.

The remarks made by Glantz and Itinarelli followed more than a decade of concerted effort on the part of a coalition of faith-based shareholders who had worked together to pressure Hollywood studios to stop showing images of smoking in youth-rated movies. This coalition included Father Mike Crosby of the Midwest Capuchin Franciscans; Cathy Rowan, a Maryknoll lay missioner and Director of Socially Responsible Investments at Trinity Health, a Catholic health care system; and Thomas McCaney and Sister Nora Nash of the Sisters of St. Francis of Philadelphia, along with As You Sow.

These are, of course, dramatic moments, notable in part because they are relatively rare. Change often comes incrementally and often takes a coordinated campaign involving building a coalition of shareholders, the media, and consumer groups.

4

How to Vote Your Proxy

Sections of this chapter are based on the 2004 handbook *Unlocking the Power of the Proxy*,[32] written by Conrad MacKerron, along with Doug Bauer and Michael Passoff. It was published by As You Sow. It remains a definitive source for information on proxy voting for foundations and endowments.

PROXY VOTING 101

Publicly traded companies are required by law to report to shareholders. They do this through a variety of means, most notably by numerous SEC filings, including an annual report, and by inviting shareholders to an annual meeting. Prior to the annual meeting, shareholders are sent documents known as proxy statements that include details about the annual meeting; ownership, board structure, and executive compensation; and other issues that will be voted on at the meeting.

The annual meeting and proxy statement provide a formal communication channel between corporate management and shareholders. At a minimum, the proxy statement asks investors to ratify issues placed on the proxy by management, such as the election of directors, the auditor report, and CEO pay package. Management may also seek approval of more complex and controversial issues, such as mergers and acquisitions, stock option plans, or resolutions brought by qualified shareholders on a variety of issues.

US Securities and Exchange Commission (SEC) rules[33] allow shareholders to file proposals with companies on corporate environmental, social, and governance issues. The requirements to file a proposal are relatively simple. Any shareholder who owns $2,000 worth of company stock and has held it for one year prior to the annual filing deadline may file a proposal. Proponents, or the shareholder(s) that file the resolution, are allowed only 500 words in the proxy statement to present their case. Management can take as much space as it would like to respond, but there is no opportunity in the proxy for proponents to respond to misleading information in the company's statement. Shareholders may object directly to the company about its response, and if it is not corrected, they may decide to bring this to the press and publish it in their own proxy briefings. These briefings can be filed with the SEC for all shareholders to access.

> THE NAME GAME: The term *proxy* means "written authorization to act in place of another." The proxy statement is the document used by companies seeking approval from shareholders on issues relating to corporate governance. The name indicates that most shareholders will be voting remotely—by proxy—rather than in person at the company's annual meeting.

SEC rules also specify issues that may not be addressed through proposals. For instance, anything relating to personal grievances or to operations that constitute less than five percent of revenue may be excluded. A company may challenge the proposal at the SEC if it thinks the proposal may be legally omitted. This is known as a "no-action" letter in which the company explains why it believes that it can omit the resolution from the proxy statement.

Many challenges relate to rules stating that issues pertaining to "ordinary business" may be excluded. However, proponents can challenge the company's logic, and if the SEC sides with the shareholder proponents, the company is very likely to place the proposal on the company proxy statement to be voted on at the annual meeting.

Proposals must receive a minimum number of votes to be allowed on the proxy the following year. Proposals must obtain three percent of the total vote their first year to be resubmitted; six percent the second year, and 10 percent its third and subsequent years. If it fails to meet these minimum votes, it may not be resubmitted for three years.

If you hold mutual funds or exchange-traded funds (ETFs) or contribute to a pension plan, you do not hold actual company shares and cannot vote by proxy directly. However, you can contact your fund manager(s) and ask them to vote in favor of issues you feel strongly about. The next chapter goes into detail about how this works.

There are four categories of votes: for, against, abstain, and not voted. This last type means that if you do not vote at all, then your votes are automatically voted by management. If you are unsure about an issue, it is best to abstain as these votes are not cast either for or against a resolution and are not counted in the final tally.

Shareholders can vote their proxies via regular mail, Internet, phone, by attending the annual meeting in person, or by having your broker or proxy service vote on your behalf. Voting instructions are provided on the proxy, and votes can be changed as long as they meet the stated deadlines (usually 24 hours before the meeting). Those attending the annual meeting in person can change or submit their votes up to the very last minute. Those who do not vote their proxies in advance may have their ballot automatically cast by brokers or management.

The critical issue is how to cast your vote. This is why every year As You Sow publishes updated *Proxy Voting Guidelines*.[34] This is different than our annual *Proxy Preview*[35] that lists every

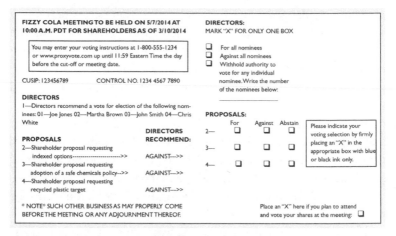

Figure 4: You can vote your proxy ballots online, by mail-in, by touch-tone phone, or have a proxy advisor take care of it for a fee. *Graphic by Tracey Fernandez Rysavy, Reprinted with permission of Green America, www.greenamerica.org.*

environmental and social resolution at every company. The guidelines lay out a progressive set of voting preferences to help you make your voting decisions. Both are referenced in the resources section at the end of the book and can be downloaded at no cost.

The key issue in deciding how to vote is truly based on your values. By reading the guidelines and understanding each issue, you can understand why the proponent has filed the resolution and why management opposes it. If you agree with the guidelines as written, you can turn these over to your proxy service or financial advisor and instruct them to follow the guidelines for all voting, or you can vote yourself.

Proxy Voting Services provide institutional and larger shareholders with professional proxy voting. Generally, individuals do their own as there is a significant cost to use one of these services. However, if you own dozens, hundreds, or even thousands of companies, it is simply too time-consuming and difficult to go online and check all the right boxes, so the service makes sense. Each vote takes time to analyze, decide, check the box, and submit.

There are two major proxy voting services: Institutional Shareholder Services Inc. (ISS)[36] and Glass Lewis[37] as well as smaller shops like Egan-Jones[38] and a personalized boutique service, Proxy Impact.[39] Each has a variety of proxy slates based on an investor's values and publishes their proxy voting guidelines for investors to review. Full disclosure—Proxy Impact collaborates with As You Sow on our annual proxy voting guidelines, which we believe are the most progressive. They are available to the public online with a link in Resources B.

How to Influence Your Fund Manager

If you do not hold equities directly but instead are invested in mutual funds or exchange-traded funds (ETF) or in a pension fund, you still have rights and can take action. The first step is to understand exactly what you own. Following are some basic definitions.

WHAT IS A MUTUAL FUND?

A mutual fund[40] is an investment vehicle that is made up of capital from many investors for the purpose of investing in a basket of securities, such as stocks, bonds, money markets, and other assets. Mutual funds are actively managed by fund managers[41] who invest the fund's capital and decide what assets to hold in an attempt to produce income for the fund's investors. A mutual fund's portfolio is structured and maintained to match the investment objectives stated in its prospectus.[42]

If you own shares in a mutual fund, you do not own the underlying stocks, bonds, and other assets. You own shares in the mutual fund itself. If you want to buy or sell shares of the fund, you put in an order, and it is executed at the close of business based on its net asset value (NAV), which is calculated at the end of every day.

WHAT IS AN EXCHANGE-TRADED FUND?

An exchange-traded fund (ETF)[43] is a marketable security that tracks an index, a commodity, bonds, or a basket of assets like an index fund.[44] Unlike mutual funds, an ETF trades like a common stock on a stock exchange. ETFs experience price changes throughout the day as they are bought and sold and typically have higher daily liquidity and lower fees than mutual funds, making them a good option for individual investors. Because it trades like a stock, an ETF does not have its net asset value calculated once at the end of every day like a mutual fund.

UNDERSTANDING YOUR 401(K) AND 403(B)

Most company-sponsored retirement plans are now online, and you can go to your account and see what mutual funds you are currently invested in. If you are not online, you should be getting a quarterly statement in the mail. These often include a pie chart showing how each contribution deducted (pre-tax) from your pay check, along with any company match, is allocated into the funds you have chosen. You can change your allocations at any time. This is your right, and you can shift your retirement savings from one fund to another and reallocate the percentage of any contributions among the funds available.

Once you identify the funds you are invested in, you can perform some due diligence on each one. Start by reading the prospectus. This is a formal legal document, required by and filed with the Securities and Exchange Commission. It should be linked to your online platform, but if not, you can search for it by name or ticker. The prospectus provides details about an investment offering for sale to the public. It lays out the basic investing philosophy of the fund and provides guidance for the fund manager, the person who buys and sells stocks, bonds, and other financial products.

ALIGN YOURSELF WITH THE FUND PHILOSOPHY

If you find that the basic investing philosophy described in the prospectus is not aligned with your values, then that's a pretty good tip-off that this may not be a fund you should be investing in. On the other hand, you may find a fund that specifically states it is designed to address a specific set of issues—for instance, to ensure gender diversity, empower women, or reduce exposure to fossil fuels. In addition, you can see if it is using ESG screens—in other words, excluding companies that do not meet certain environmental, social, and governance guidelines. Also look to see if it is focused on big companies (large-cap) or smaller ones (small-cap) that may be more volatile and therefore offer more risk but also more possible gain. All of these are laid out in the prospectus. Also, check to see if it is diversified.[45] This means that it holds stocks and bonds from a broad range of sectors. For instance, an undiversified fund may be focused only on information technology but not on industrials, telecommunications, or healthcare.

WHAT IF NONE OF THE FUNDS OFFERED IN YOUR PLAN MATCH YOUR VALUES?

A prospectus is a good place to start to understand basic philosophy. However, if you want to see exact holdings, you will need other tools, as the prospectus generally will only show the top 10 holdings. It's nearly impossible to know exactly what a fund holds at any given moment, because mutual fund managers may buy and sell stocks at any time, and they only report to the SEC once a quarter, and the SEC only publishes it to their public database once a year. Even if you search long and hard to find every holding in a fund, the search will likely be out of date.

However, there are new tools to help you do this, and we devote chapter 12 to a detailed tour of some of these tools to help you see the gender diversity of corporate boards and the fossil fuel holdings of companies within the most-held funds.

Your company-sponsored retirement plan will probably have approximately 15 to 40 funds to pick from. These are generally a variety of large-cap, small-cap, international, bonds, and other types of mutual funds and ETFs. However, many of these funds do not use ESG principles at all; only recently have new funds been offered focused on gender equity, LGBT rights, human rights, and other issues. Few are fossil-free. This means that if you want specific funds offered to you and the rest of the employees at your company, you will need to talk to your plan administrator. Chapter 13 is devoted to a step-by-step guide about how to approach your plan administrator to request that new offerings be added to align with your values.

HOW FUNDS VOTE THEIR PROXIES

The Employee Retirement Income Security Act (ERISA) is a federal law that was enacted to protect the interests of employee benefit plan participants and their beneficiaries. It establishes minimum standards for pension plans and provides rules for employee benefit plans. While ERISA does not specifically lay out fiduciary responsibilities regarding proxy voting, the Department of Labor does consider the voting of proxies a fiduciary act of the management of the plan.[46] Proxies are considered an asset of the plan and need to be voted in a manner that supports the shareholders of the company.[47] There are also rules stating that it is the plan trustee who must decide how to vote. The bottom line is that they must vote, and how they do tells a lot about how the fund aligns with your values.

Online tools like Proxy Democracy[48] track selected mutual fund voting on a range of ESG issues. You can also go to the fund sites and see their voting history. This is very telling, as a fund that basically rubber-stamps management on excessive CEO pay, does not support fair labor and human rights, and votes against climate disclosure on its shareholder proxy resolutions may not be aligned with your values.

Many pension funds also display their voting records on their websites. If they don't, you can call your fund managers and ask for this information. Challenging how your money is invested in pension funds is difficult. First of all, pension funds generally own the entire market. Also, they have detailed procedures to make sure that they do not violate their fiduciary duty. If their investing philosophy is not in alignment with your values, you can talk to their staff to find out how to work your request through the proper channels. If enough pensioners sign letters, show up at investment committee meetings, and follow the prescribed process for change, you will get a fair hearing, and the pension fund may integrate your thinking into their future plans. It was this kind of pressure that got the world's largest pension fund, NORGES to divest from coal.[49]

CHAPTER

6

Engaging With a Company and Filing a Shareholder Resolution

As a shareholder, if you feel that a corporation in which you have invested is doing something harmful and it fits within the environmental, social, and governance concerns as described above, one way to address your concern is to engage directly with the company in a collaborative way. By doing this, you can work through the process with them to understand why they have such a policy or have taken such an action, and if your engagement is not successful, you can file a resolution. Here is a hypothetical example to illustrate the step-by-step process of bringing about change in a company you own as an investor.

Requirements: You must own $2,000 worth of stock that you have held for one year prior to the filing deadline. You must commit to not selling the stock until after the annual meeting. It must also be a voting class of stock,[50] as some classes of stock do not have the right to vote or file resolutions. There are minimum vote thresholds that also must be met for filing in subsequent years. Resolutions must obtain three percent of the total vote their first year to be resubmitted, six percent the second year, and 10 percent the third year and all subsequent years. If it fails to meet these vote levels, it may not be resubmitted for three years.

YOU OWN STOCK DIRECTLY

Remember your dog that got under the fence? Let's say that he has formed a corporation called Puppy, Inc. It has four product lines: dog apparel, dog treats, dog flea collars, and dog toys. You trust him, and he seems to have a good management team, so a year ago you purchased $2,000 worth of their stock, and over the past year it has gone up in value. The importance of the amount of this investment, the fact that it has not lost value, and the period of time you have held it will become apparent later.

The company seems to understand its customer base. It has a diverse board made up not only of pure-bred shepherds, terriers, and sporting dogs, but also a good portion of mutts. Its products are selling well. So far, this seems like a great investment.

Figure 5: Puppy, Inc. looked like a great investment. *Used with permission of As You Sow, the author, and iStock Photos.*

YOU HAVE AN ISSUE WITH SOME COMPANY POLICIES

One day, you come across an article with information leaked from inside Puppy, Inc. that describes cotton harvested for dog vests by child slave labor in Uzbekistan. It is also using nanomaterials in the coloring of their dog treats. The flea collar division has been charged with environmental violations for discharging toxins into their waste water. Furthermore, the plastic toys have been shown by a watchdog group to contain lead, people claim that their puppies have lost IQ points, and litigation is pending.

You do some research and see that other groups are filing shareholder resolutions on the nanomaterials, the toxic discharges, and the lead. You decide to focus on the human rights issue. You realize that, as a shareholder, one reason for concern is that if Puppy, Inc. is truly involved, customers would stop buying their products, and the company's value would be impacted. There goes your $2,000 investment.

Figure 6: Puppy, Inc. management made some poor business decisions. *Used with permission of As You Sow, the author, and iStock Photos*

YOU CONTACT THE COMPANY

Your concern is significant enough that you decide to take the first step, which is to call the company. The best place to start is to download and read the corporate social responsibility (CSR) report and contact the CSR department. If there is no report or CSR staff then try investor relations (IR). In one possible scenario a polite person directs you to the company's legal department where an attorney thanks you for your concern. You are assured that a full review of the company's policies has been launched, modifications subsequently made, damaged parties' restitutions have been settled, and the managers in charge of these violations have been reprimanded or fired. This is all completely satisfactory to you.

However, even if you represent a large institutional investor like a pension fund or major mutual fund, you may get only a polite conversation. It may be that the people who you talk to want to help, but they have little power to make change, and Puppy, Inc. is a big company. Like a great ship, changing a company's course takes time and planning. So, you take step two: putting your concerns in writing.

You might address your letter to the CEO, in care of the investor relations department. Point out that you have been a satisfied shareholder up until now, and then detail your concerns, particularly as they affect the value of your investment.

Then you wait. You can imagine that the CEO of a major corporation with multiple crises pending is fairly busy, so you need to be patient. Finally, a letter bearing the distinctive Puppy, Inc. logo appears in your mailbox. Eagerly, you tear it open, and are disappointed that it is a canned response referring you to the policy statement on their website. If you're lucky, your name will be spelled correctly, but in terms of addressing your concerns, the company has done exactly nothing.

Often joint investor letters are organized by socially responsible investment groups or by convening organizations such as Ceres and the Interfaith Center on Corporate Responsibility (ICCR). These letters are generally written by one organization or in collaboration. Getting many investors to sign on brings institutions together that may have in aggregate tens or hundreds of billions of dollars in assets under management (AUM). Sometimes the pension funds join them as well, and the assets get into the trillions of dollars. It's important to note that it's critical to be part of a coalition, both for coordination and for increased impact.

So far, you haven't expended a great deal of time or effort on getting Puppy, Inc. to change. But you really believe that your concerns are important and are willing to do what's necessary to make sure your voice is heard.

YOU DECIDE TO CO-FILE OR FILE A SHAREHOLDER RESOLUTION

Although the process of submitting a shareholder resolution seems intimidating, you can accomplish it as an individual. However, it can be a time-consuming process, and there are bureaucratic as well as logistical hurdles to clear. Most shareholders partner with a socially responsible investing firm or shareholder advocacy organization that handles the technical requirements. If you choose that path, all the shareholders have to do is authorize them to file on their behalf and have their broker provide a proof of ownership letter.

However, for the sake of illustration, let's say you're going to take on the challenge yourself. The fact is, as we'll see later on, shareholder resolutions can achieve significant results, even if they do not go to a vote at the annual meeting. However, most often it will take patience and tenacity to bring about significant and lasting change at one company and even more effort to transform an entire industry.

After doing some research, you learn that, according to SEC rules, any shareholder who has held a minimum of $2,000 worth of company stock for one year prior to the annual filing deadline may file a shareholder resolution. You decide you may want to file a shareholder resolution asking the board of Puppy, Inc. to publicly explain company labor policies, what the potential financial impact is to shareholders if the child slave labor allegations are true, and how the company intends to become a leader on resolving this issue.

The first step is to see what other groups are doing in this area. Has anyone else filed with Puppy, Inc. on this issue? Has anyone filed on this issue with another company? Has anyone filed with Puppy, Inc. on other issues? If so, what happened? If someone has filed, you can find a basic description of the resolution and often a sidebar by the proponent by looking at *Proxy Preview*, available free at www.proxypreview.org. It is published by As You Sow in collaboration with partners Sustainable Investments Institute[51] (Si2), and Proxy Impact.[52] For more detailed information on recent proxy proposals at a company, you should review annual proxy filings and 8-K reports required to be filed with the SEC. The simplest way is to use rankandfiled.com,[53] which puts SEC data in a simple interface; use the SEC database; or Google a company name, year, and the words "proxy statement." This is all public information and readily available.

COORDINATION WITH OTHER ADVOCATES IS CRITICAL

It is very important that you do your basic research. If you were to file a resolution that is similar to one that has been filed by another group, then the company can exclude one or the other for redundancy. This may disrupt an advocate who has been working on an issue at a specific company for years and could seriously hinder progress. The importance of coordination with other shareholder advocates cannot be overstated.

You may find that other advocates have filed on this very issue for multiple years and have gotten strong votes and are negotiating with Puppy, Inc. at this very moment. If this is the case, you can contact those advocates and ask to join the coalition to be kept in the loop. You may find that there has been a filing that was withdrawn last year after a dialogue.

If multiple advocates are filing on the same issue, there will generally be one lead filer. This is not a legal distinction but is a widespread practice that shareholders use when working together. The lead filer is usually responsible for drafting the resolution, leading the dialogue(s), defending the no-action letter with the SEC, and negotiating withdrawal if there is one. Co-filers are shareholders that range from being deeply active with the resolution and dialogue, to simply piggybacking on the work of the lead filer. They submit the exact same resolution with a letter stating that they are co-filing. There is no limit to the number of co-filers on a resolution, and if there are many, it sends a signal to the company that this is a serious issue. Co-filers agree to follow the lead filer's decisions.

Therefore, before you start to write your own resolution, make sure that you know if there has been a similar resolution filed in the past, and if so, contact the lead filer and see what is going on. If the advocates are preparing to file again, most likely you will be invited to join the coalition as a co-filer. If this is the case, you can save yourself a great deal of work and be part of a group that is working to make the same changes. See the Resource section at the end of the book for a list of key contacts and web links.

Other important research you should do is finding out if the company is closely held, meaning that management holds a vast majority, or if the shares held by management have a 10X or 100X voting preference. This means that even if you got every other shareholder to vote yes on your resolution, every management vote counts as 100, and you would never get above the three percent SEC minimum threshold. This may impact your strategy and decision to file.

THE REQUIREMENTS FOR SUBMITTING A SHAREHOLDER RESOLUTION

You've done your homework, and you are not going to step on anyone else's toes. You believe that your shareholder resolution complies with the fairly stringent SEC rules, and if you file,

Puppy, Inc. will put it on the company's proxy statement to be voted on at the AGM.

Your next step is to find the filing deadline for shareholder resolutions in the company's proxy statement from the previous year. Generally, the filing deadline is six months prior to the annual general meeting. Your filing packet must be in the company's possession prior to the close of business (their local time) on the filing deadline. Be sure to check that the filing deadline has not been set on a national holiday or weekend when mail is not delivered—if they do not have your resolution in hand, it may be excluded.

The good news is that you meet the SEC's first criterion: you have owned a minimum of $2,000 worth of Puppy, Inc. stock for a calendar year prior to the filing deadline. Double check that the total value has not dipped below that amount 60 days prior to filing. Also, you must commit to maintaining ownership of that stock through the date of the company's annual general meeting.

You should be aware that a few corporations issue different classes of stock. Verify that your shares have voting rights— sometimes class A has voting rights; sometimes it's class B. Each company has different rules, and it's important to make sure. If you have the wrong class, you cannot file a resolution or vote. To continue, you would have to buy some stock that did have voting rights and wait another year before you'd be eligible to file.

DRAFTING A SHAREHOLDER RESOLUTION

If you found an advocacy organization or another filer working on this issue and decided to co-file with them, let them do the work of drafting and vetting the resolution. As co-filers they may share early versions with you and may offer to do the filing for you as well. Or they will send you the final version of the resolution prior to the filing deadline so you can submit it yourself, noting in the cover letter that you are co-filing with another group.

If you are writing your own resolution, then you will need to understand that the SEC has set specific criteria for shareholder resolutions, and failure to meet any of them may be grounds for rejection. For example, your resolution cannot address the "ordinary business" of the company. Don't ask Puppy, Inc. to offer new vest styles or chew-toy flavors. Also, your resolution may not contain any false or misleading statements. Claiming that adopting your resolution would lead to a 500 percent increase in sales would be possible grounds for rejection if the company could show that this is not true.

Finally, you must be concise: the statement is limited to 500 words. Achieving this is trickier than just clicking the "word count" button on your computer. For one, acronyms may be counted as though they are written out. "*SEC*," for example, may be counted as four words: *Securities and Exchange Commission.* Also, numbers can count as though they were written out. For example, "*42%*" would count as three words: *forty-two percent.* Words with dashes are not one word. It pays to be a stickler for detail because you don't want to give Puppy, Inc. or the SEC any grounds to reject your resolution on technical grounds.

The best way to start is to read other shareholder resolutions, those that made it through an SEC challenge or that the company did not challenge because they felt they would lose. These are all in the public record and easily accessible.

There are thousands of resolutions that can be found online. They are all catalogued in the SEC's database, the Electronic Data Gathering Analysis and Retrieval system[54] (EDGAR). To access the EDGAR database, go to the SEC's website, www.sec.gov, and find the tab entitled "Filings (EDGAR)." Click on "Company Filings Search." When you get to the screen entitled "EDGAR Company Filings," you can enter a company name or stock ticker to see all of the filings, including last year's proxy statement.[55]

To view the annual proxy statement, select the most recent filing that has the title "DEF 14A," short for "definitive," or final, proxy statement. "14A" refers to the fact that proxy statements are filed pursuant to Section 14(a) of the Securities Exchange Act of 1934. Proxy statements are also often accessible via the investor relations section of a company's website. The proxy statement provides the text of each proposal and the company's statement in response; an 8-K form filed shortly after each annual meeting may also be accessed, which provides voting results.

You can also search databases of recently filed proposals at organizations including Ceres and As You Sow that are searchable by company/issue/year.[56, 57] Another way, so you don't have to look through all of a company's filings, is to Google the company name; for example, if you were looking for Kroger supermarkets, you would search, "Kroger, Proxy Statement 2015."[58]

In this case, to read the resolutions you would go to page 57. Kroger had several in 2015: one asking for a report on the environmental impacts of continuing to use unrecyclable packaging, one asking for a study of policy options that could reduce or eliminate routine antibiotic use in the production of its private label brand meats, and one asking for an assessment on human rights. In the sidebar I have included the full text of two resolutions as examples.

The first example is a human rights resolution that starts with a "Resolved" clause and then has a supporting statement. More often you will find three sections as in the second example antibiotic resolution. First there is the "Whereas" clause. This is where you lay out your case: "Whereas Puppy, Inc. may have human rights violations in its supply chain and does not have a policy on this issue." Cite other companies that have a strong policy and examples of negative brand impact such as media stories on abusive practices to make your case that this issue could impact sales and therefore incur shareholder risk and a material reason for concern.

Next is the "resolved" clause. This is what you want the company to do. Often you ask for a report detailing the negative impact to the brand or negative impact to shareholder value because of some activity. The report should be required by a specific and workable date. A standard phrase to make the request reasonable for the company to fulfill is, "Such report should be prepared at reasonable cost, omitting confidential information." Keep in mind that the SEC is less likely to reject, and shareholders are more likely to vote for, proposals asking the company to study and report on making a desired policy change than asking directly for that change.

RESOLUTION EXAMPLE ONE

Human Rights Risk Assessment—2015
Filed by The Sisters of St. Francis Philadelphia

RESOLVED, that shareholders of The Kroger Company ("Kroger") urge the Board to report to shareholders, at reasonable cost and omitting proprietary information, on Kroger's process for identifying and analyzing potential and actual human rights risks of Kroger's operations and supply chain (referred to herein as a "human rights risk assessment") addressing the following:

- Human rights principles used to frame the assessment

- Frequency of assessment

- Methodology used to track and measure performance

- Nature and extent of consultation with relevant stakeholders in connection with assessment

- How the results of the assessments are incorporated into company policies and decision making.

The report should be made available to shareholders on Kroger's website no later than October 31, 2015.

Supporting Statement

As long-term shareholders, we favor policies and practices that protect and enhance the value of our investments. There is increasing recognition that company risks related to human rights violations, such as litigation, reputational damage, and project delays and disruptions, can adversely affect shareholder value.

Kroger, like many other companies, has adopted a supplier code of conduct

(See: The Kroger Company Standard Vendor Agreement) but has yet to publish a company-wide Human Rights Policy, addressing human rights issues and a separate human rights code that applies to its suppliers. Adoption of these principles would be an important first step in effectively managing human rights risks. Companies must then assess risks to shareholder value of human rights practices in their operations and supply chains to translate principles into protective practices.

The importance of human rights risk assessment is reflected in the United Nations Guiding Principles on Business and Human Rights (the "Ruggie Principles") approved by the UN Human Rights Council in 2011. The Ruggie Principles urge that "business enterprises should carry out human rights due diligence . . . accessing actual and potential human rights impacts, integrating and acting upon the findings, tracking responses, and communicating how impacts are addressed" (http://www.business-humanrights. org/media/documents/ruggie/ruggie-guiding-principles-21-mar-2011.pdf).

Kroger's business exposes it to significant human rights risks. As of year-end 2012, Kroger operations, including supermarkets, convenience and jewelry stores, are located in over 40 states, with suppliers in countries around the world, including Iran, China, and Malaysia. The company's supply chain is complex and global and unsuccessful labor negotiations, supply chain interruptions and civil unrest could adversely affect the company's ability to execute its strategic plan.

We urge shareholders to vote for this proposal.

RESOLUTION EXAMPLE TWO

Antibiotic Use in Factory Farming—2015

Filed by As You Sow

Whereas: Antibiotic resistance has become a public health crisis. 'Superbugs'—bacteria immune or resistant to one or more antibiotics—infect over 2 million people in the U.S. and kill over 23,000 annually, according to the Centers for Disease Control and Prevention. As resistance increases, medications used to treat human infections lose their effectiveness, leading the World Health Organization to warn of "a post-antibiotic era."

An important cause of antibiotic resistant bacteria is the overuse of antibiotics in food-animal production, for the routine, non-therapeutic purposes of promoting faster growth or preventing (instead of treating) illness. In the U.S., more than 70% of medically important antibiotics are sold for use on food-animals.

Calls to restrict or ban the routine use of medically important antibiotics for food-animals have been endorsed by the American Medical Association, American Public Health Association, and other leading health organizations:

Eating food contaminated with antibiotic resistant bacteria is one way in which superbugs can be transmitted from a farm to human population. Government testing of raw supermarket meat detected 'superbug' versions of salmonella, E. coli, or other bacteria in 81% of ground turkey, 55% of ground beef, and 39% of chicken sampled.

An outbreak of antibiotic-resistant Salmonella from chicken last year resulted in more than 600 known illnesses. Several Kroger private brand chicken products were recalled by Foster Farms as part of this outbreak.

A 2012 Consumer Reports survey concluded that the majority of consumers surveyed were extremely or very concerned about the use of antibiotics in animal feed and would spend more for meat produced without these drugs.

Companies including Whole Foods, Panera Bread, Chipotle, and Chik-fil-A have policies against purchasing meat produced with antibiotics, heightening the risks to companies not acting on this issue. Perdue Foods announced that it has phased out routine antibiotic use in the production of its chicken meat, demonstrating that meat can be produced on a large scale without overusing antibiotics.

Kroger is one of the largest supermarket chains in the nation, with perishable food including meat and deli items accounting for around 21% of the company's revenue in 2013. Consequently, food quality and safety trends should be of top priority to the company. Kroger faces reputational risk and liability concerns if it sells meat containing antibiotic resistant bacteria.

Resolved: Shareholders request that the Board undertake and publish a study of policy options that could reduce or eliminate routine antibiotic use in the production of its private label brand meats.

Supporting Statement:

Proponents suggest that the Board explore policy options such as the following: adopt a time-bound plan to phase out purchases of meat produced with routine antibiotic use; establish a new procurement policy that gives preference to suppliers that meet these standards; public declaration of such preferences. "Routine antibiotic use" means using antibiotics, on food animals, that belong to the same classes of drugs administered to humans, for the non-therapeutic purposes of growth promotion or disease prevention."

The third section is optional and is a "Supporting Statement." This generally provides a summary and details of what a successful report will contain. Find a resolution that matches as closely as possible to your issue and read several that made it to a vote before you start.

There is a great deal of expertise that goes into drafting a resolution. Proponents work diligently to make every one of the 500 words in each resolution count. Each phrase is well researched and carefully crafted.

Many shareholder advocates have their resolution reviewed by an attorney familiar with the SEC's previous rulings to decrease the possibility that a challenge will result, leading to the resolution being omitted. It is important to have your facts and analysis completely accurate in these public documents. You should be aware that corporate attorneys will be looking for any reason to ask the SEC to not allow the resolution to go to a vote. In fact, many companies challenge resolutions whether there is cause or not, and there are many examples of an individual shareholder writing to the SEC directly to defend a resolution and prevailing over large corporate law firms that assumed a counterbrief would not be filed.

READY TO SUBMIT

When you are ready to file, draft a cover letter to the attention of the corporate secretary that includes your contact information and some very specific required language. If you are co-filing, add the name of the lead filer to the language below.

- The resolution you are submitting is "for inclusion in the proxy statement in accordance with Rule 14a-8 of the general rules and regulations of the Securities Exchange Act of 1934."

- You or a representative "will attend the annual meeting to move the resolution as required by SEC rules."

- You "are the beneficial owner of XX number of shares of Puppy, Inc. common stock."
- You "have held the requisite amount of stock for over a year and intend to maintain ownership through the annual meeting" of the year in question.

PROOF OF OWNERSHIP

Last, you need to acquire a verification of stock ownership or proof of ownership letter. This is typically a letter signed by your broker. It must indicate that you have owned the stock continuously for at least a year prior to your submission. Note that some brokers can get you this letter in a few days, and others take weeks and often have delays. Most notably E*TRADE, USAA, and Schwab have proven to have more complex systems for shareholders to traverse in obtaining this required document. Be assured that acquiring it is your legal right, and your brokers *must* produce this letter. Be certain to leave enough lead time.

SUBMISSION

Just to be on the safe side, mail or overnight the whole package with a signature required on delivery and retain the receipt. Some companies have started to accept email delivery. Contact the corporate secretary well in advance to ask if you can submit via email, send it with a delivery receipt and ask for a confirmation email."

You have now gotten to the starting line of the real engagement to press for change. In the next chapter we will delve into the next steps and onward to the annual general meeting!

Alan Farago lives in South Florida. He writes for *Huffington Post* and co-blogs "Eye on Miami," a well-regarded blog on local and state political and environmental issues. One of his favorite spots to visit is Biscayne National Park, which is threatened by the malfunctioning cooling canal system serving two nuclear reactors at Turkey Point. About five years ago Florida Power & Light (FPL) announced plans for two new nuclear plants at the same location, surrounded by some of the lowest-lying lands in Florida.

Since the mid-1990s the issue of sea level rise has been on people's minds in South Florida. Streets, garages, and sewer systems are vulnerable. The City of Miami Beach is in the midst of a $500 million effort to harden its sewage system from sea level rise. According to Alan, "You have a scenario where lots of people are asking common-sense questions. Why would a company like FPL put $20 billion of assets into an area that will be flooded in a few decades? Is this in the best interest of ratepayers?"

Therefore, a few years ago Alan and his wife, Lisa, decided to ask questions directly to the company about sea-level rise. They purchased stock in NextEra Energy, Inc., the parent company of FPL, to file a shareholder resolution. The purpose of the resolution was to focus public and investor attention on a subject that management did not want to talk about.

Although he now owned the stock, he did not fully understand the SEC requirement to hold shares for a year. In the interim, many new peer-reviewed articles on sea-level rise were published.

"I did not know first thing about writing a proposal to pass SEC muster, but there is a lot of information available in the public record to use as a model." He reviewed other resolutions on climate change, and although none dealt specifically with sea-level rise, he began to understand what was required. The company got his resolution and did not call, so there was no dialogue. However, they did file a no-action letter with the SEC to prevent the resolution from coming to a vote. Alan read their letter and changed some wording on his resolution so it would not appear to be micro-managing and sent it to the SEC. A few weeks later he found out that he won, and it would go to a vote.

Although NextEra reached out to meet, Alan said, "I wanted this to come to a vote. I understood the chances of a nonbinding resolution on the environment were slim, but somehow there has to be a way to hold corporations accountable for climate change impacts that already are here and now. The resolution calls into question whether FPL should even be planning a nuclear reactor—I am actually not against nuclear—it's just the worst place in the country to spend $20 billion of ratepayer money. It is time for a national conversation on sea-level rise. The tectonic plates are shifting, and I hope that our proposal is part of making this change." Alan's resolution won a 35 percent vote and we may see more sea-level rise resolutions in the years to come.

7

Opportunities and Decisions to Make Real Change

You have now entered the phase of direct engagement with a public company, and there are many twists and turns in the road ahead. There will be decision points along the way, and each is an opportunity to stay true to your purpose and keep the long-term impact that you want as the focus of your efforts.

There are also many SEC guidelines and rules that will shape the form of the interaction with the company. After sending in your resolution and paperwork, you will probably have to wait at least a few weeks for the company to respond. If the company does not challenge your resolution, it should appear on the proxy ballot. However, as mentioned before, management may formally submit a "no-action letter" to the SEC, which requests that the resolution be rejected on technical or legal grounds.

Most likely the company will contact you and ask you to discuss withdrawing the resolution. There could be any number of reasons for this. For example, they might already have changed their cotton suppliers and stopped using material sourced by known human rights violators. In other words, they may have already directly addressed your concerns. Or, the board of directors might want to avoid raising the issue with shareholders and the press and publicly admitting that they've committed such a massive oversight. Naturally, you agree to a meeting, because it is a chance to present your case. Generally these are by conference call, although they can be also face to face.

When that day arrives, you are prepared. You have the text of your resolution, your rationale for why it is important, and all the research and data you've amassed in support of your cause.

THE WITHDRAWAL DIALOGUE

If you have co-filed, the withdrawal dialogue will be run by the lead filer, who may invite you to attend as an observer. If you want to participate, you should talk to the lead filer in advance so that your comments are in alignment, the agenda is set, and you know when it is your turn to speak.

Assuming that you are the lead filer and leading the dialogue, you should know that several things could happen at the meeting. Ideally, the company will tell you it has decided to implement all of the changes you suggest. In consideration of this, you generously offer to withdraw the resolution so long as they publicly state their planned changes along with a credible timeline. That way, if they do not make the promised changes, you have a reason to refile the resolution the following year. In addition, you have the option to make your case in the media that Puppy, Inc. does not keep their promises. This is something that their customers care about. By all measures, this is a sweet victory—but it is not common. Generally, if the company was ready to make the change, it would have happened in the dialogue before you filed.

A more likely scenario is that the company offers to implement some, but not all, of the changes you suggest. In that case, you have to decide whether partial implementation is substantive progress that will lead to the desired change and whether it is worthwhile devoting more time and resources to continuing forward with your resolution.

The company may also offer neither complete nor partial implementation of your resolution. You may be told that your concerns are unfounded, the allegations were incorrect, the suppliers they use have top-tier human rights and labor practices, or you don't really understand the market or the competition. It may tell you that your resolution will be challenged at the SEC and that they will prevail. In effect, you may get a pat on the head and be shown the door, calculating, perhaps, that your resolution is fundamentally flawed or you really don't have what it takes to push your resolution over the finish line.

The corporation may also tell you that even if your resolution goes to a vote and is supported by a significant number of shareholders, it has absolutely no intention of implementing any change. After all, in general, shareholder resolutions are nonbinding (the legal term is "precatory"). So it may tell you to save all the time, money, and aggravation of promoting the resolution and go your merry way.

However the corporation plays it, don't give up easily. You wouldn't be at the table if the corporate executives didn't feel that your request had some validity. But your goal as a shareholder is not to try and strong-arm the corporation into agreeing with you. Your goal is to make your resolution bring about change in the real world. Assuming that the allegations are true based on the assumption that you already double-checked and had them validated by a third party, the best path forward is to present a win-win scenario to reduce risk to the company and make the change you desire.

WHO HAS THE POWER IN THE NEGOTIATION?

That depends on the precise circumstances, but both parties—the shareholder and the corporation—have power. As a shareholder, you have the power of ownership. A corporation has the power to listen politely and then ignore you but possibly face consumer backlash, a devalued brand, and increased risk. The more coordination you do to build a coalition of shareholders and the more convincing your data and presentation is, the stronger your hand will be. Don't forget that you have time on your side. Companies, where possible, would like to resolve issues before the day they print the proxy ballot.

HOW TO PRESENT YOUR CASE

Recent social science research conducted at the University of Toronto[59, 60] indicates that coming in, rhetorical guns blazing with passion, is exactly the wrong route. Passion, the study showed, revs up those already committed to the cause, but it does not persuade your opponents.

The best approach is to use arguments that speak to the intersection of your concerns and the company's. In other words, be honest and offer a business case that is a win-win. Naturally, at the top of the list in terms of its appeal to business people is profit. Your argument should demonstrate that your resolution will improve the bottom line and simultaneously reduce risk for the company and shareholders.

Even if your proposal is going to cost money to implement, the bottom line is the bottom line. However, as in the case of the McDonald's foam cup program, which did cost money to implement, public perception plays strongly on the minds of business people. Consumers want to patronize a company that is behaving responsibly. Toward that end, the corporation can trumpet its behavior and win loyalty and new customers. This has bottom-line value of new customers, plus earned media is far less expensive than paying for advertising. So there is a calculation involved, and the more you have thought this through, the better.

Perhaps your program, though it may be a continuing expense, has the potential to improve public perception of the corporation to such a degree that its markets will expand, investors will be attracted, and in time the extra costs will be more than compensated for. Studies have shown that brand perception can be calculated in dollars. Fortune and Bell Pottinger states that, "A study of FTSE 250 companies shows that, on average, reputation accounts for 27 percent of a company's market capitalization."[61] Do the math: you are negotiating for a lot of value.

A GREENER APPLE

A classic example of a negotiation with a notoriously tough corporation that was quite heated (but ended up with a positive change) took place leading up to May 2, 2007, when Apple CEO, Steve Jobs, made the public statement on the Apple website, "Today is the first time we have openly discussed our plans to become a greener Apple. It will not be the last. We apologize for leaving you in the dark for so long."[62]

This was the first time that Apple had publicly addressed the issues of electronics waste and hazardous materials. How did this change come about? Jobs's reputation as a corporate leader that refused input from anyone—especially his shareholders—is famous. Yet, this announcement came shortly after shareholder resolutions on electronic waste were filed and he had a meeting with the lead proponents. What happened in that negotiation?

Some background first: as the information age got into full swing, it became apparent that a mountain of electronic waste (e-waste) was forming. The manufacture of one computer workstation required more than 700 chemical compounds, about half of which were hazardous, including arsenic, brominated flame retardants, cadmium, hexavalent chromium, lead, and mercury. Tens of millions of computers, monitors, and cell phones were being discarded every year, most headed straight to the landfill even though they contained valuable precious metals like gold and silver, as well as problematic ones like lead and cadmium that leached into the water and air.

Pioneering work by Basel Action Network[63] revealed that large quantities of obsolete electronics were exported to China and Nigeria for "recycling," which often meant dumping e-waste in areas where a few valuable materials were extracted by poor people using primitive methods in a manner that posed a threat to their health. Workers openly burned plastic wiring and circuit boards to obtain copper, gold, and silver, producing harmful fumes. Tons of residual materials deemed not to have economic value lay strewn around the area, polluting local rivers.

As You Sow's work on e-waste began in 2003, led by Senior Vice President Conrad MacKerron, who formed a coalition of SRI allies including Calvert, Green Century, Pax, and Walden Asset Management to press major brands like Dell, Hewlett-Packard (HP), IBM, and Apple to set e-waste take-back goals.

Dell, already under pressure from a grass roots campaign, committed to a take-back goal in 2004. Later that year HP, which had an initial take-back program operating, accelerated its goal, pledging to recycle one billion pounds of e-waste by 2007.

But Apple, in the process of moving from innovative creator of the Mac to a global electronics powerhouse dominating the personal electronics market, was typically silent and not open to dialogue. MacKerron reached out to former Vice President Al Gore, who was on the Apple board. Several shareholder proposals were filed. Still, there was no progress. Finally, at the 2006 shareholder meeting, Executive Director Larry Fahn was able to engage Steve Jobs in a friendly discussion as the resolution was presented, and Jobs agreed to meet and see if progress could be made. The shareholder proposal asking Apple to improve its e-waste policies received a decent vote of 10 percent of shares voted.

The meeting with Jobs would not occur until almost another year passed. In February 2007 MacKerron, Fahn, research associate Nishita Bakshi, and As You Sow board chair Thomas Van Dyck met with Jobs in his Cupertino office. True to form, Jobs offered brilliant insights but was also caustic, at times berating his visitors for overstepping their boundaries and railing against Greenpeace, which had launched a campaign for Apple to phase out toxins in its components, before acknowledging the recycling problem. The shareholder team held firm that an e-waste take-back policy was good for Apple and that competitors were way ahead.

At one point, Jobs dismissively tossed a presentation the group's staff had spent weeks preparing back across the table at them. It was time to improvise. Van Dyck and other team members launched into a series of questions during the meeting to find out where his top concerns were. They recall asking Jobs if he believed having a greener Apple would sell more products. He said no. The team asked, if Apple was perceived as an environmental laggard, might it sell less products? Jobs said, yes. He felt that his shareholders, employees, and community deserved better from Apple, and he wanted to beat his competitor Michael Dell of Dell Computers, which had already announced strong electronic waste take-back goals. The team saw that he was frustrated by Dell as a competitor, and despite his ire, by the end of the meeting, Jobs agreed to develop a strong recycling commitment. Three months later, the company announced goals as part of a broad set of environmental commitments known as "A Greener Apple."

The move came just a week before shareholders would have voted on another resolution asking Apple to report on improving e-waste take-back efforts, underscoring the importance of shareholder pressure. As You Sow withdrew the proposal in acknowledgement of the company's commitments, and an uncharacteristically chastened Jobs apologized to shareholders for not previously sharing its environmental policy plans when he was quoted in *Waste News*, on May 14, 2007: "It is generally not Apple's policy to trumpet our plans for the future. Unfortunately, this policy has left our customers, shareholders, employees, and the industry in the dark about Apple's desires and plans to become greener. So today we are changing our policy."[64]

WHEN TO END NEGOTIATIONS

Naturally, every negotiation is different, but as Kenny Rogers sings in "The Gambler," "You gotta know when to hold 'em, know when to fold 'em." Asking for too much out of moral indignation may result in getting nothing. Ask for too little, and you may leave the meeting bitterly disappointed. Timing is also very important. As you approach the deadline for no-action letters to be filed, for the proxy to be printed, and for the annual meeting, you can expect negotiations to heat up. These are three opportunities to withdraw the resolution in exchange for some progress.

Also, you are dealing with people. If you are unreasonable or obnoxious, they may not want to deal with you at all. If you present a well-thought-through business opportunity for the company to improve its brand, its disclosures, its policies, and its bottom line, you may come to an agreement and withdraw. Remember that companies cannot change practices on a dime. Current procedures and practices will need to be reviewed and possibly changed,

The Material World: The concept of what is "material," in the legal and business sense, is at the heart of much of what shareholder advocates do on behalf of investors. Under US Securities and Exchange Commission (SEC) rules, *material information* must be disclosed to investors.[65] The Sustainability Accounting Standards Board (SASB) has brought together industry experts to establish definitions of materiality and how to account for them. SASB standards are voluntary and claim to be "the only standards designed to support disclosure of material sustainability information in a cost-effective, decision-useful way."[66]

If shareholders ask a company for information, say, about carbon asset risk, the company may claim the information is not "material," and withhold it. The US Supreme Court defines "material" information as presenting "a substantial likelihood that the disclosure of the omitted fact would have been viewed by the reasonable investor as having significantly altered the 'total mix' of information made available."[67] The Court recently reaffirmed this definition.[68]

Note that the Court's focus is on the "reasonable investor," not the reasonable company, as some have mistakenly interpreted. The corporation is obligated to include material information in its annual report and other periodic filings; thus, shareholders can ask for disclosures that alter the "total mix of information" to make a buy or sell decision on a given stock.

research will need to be conducted, various stakeholders within and outside the company will need to be consulted, contracts with vendors may need to run their course, and trials may need to be implemented. Progress may be slower than what you would like, and the realities of changing a large corporation means that you want it implemented in a robust and thoughtful way so that the change can withstand the test of time. Your negotiations and expectations should account for this reality.

HOW DOES THE SEC RESOLVE NO-ACTION CHALLENGES?

If a company chooses to not take action (no-action) on the request for a resolution to be placed on the proxy, one of the main ways they do this is to challenge the proposal as "substantially implemented." If you file a resolution asking for a report on greenhouse gas emissions and the company writes a no-action letter to the SEC showing that a report satisfying the request is publicly available on its website, then you will need to make the case that you were aware of the report but that it is insufficient, and even then you may not win.

Some companies create marginal reports that are just good enough to appear to disclose "material information," but not quite enough to be really useful to a shareholder making a business decision. So the argument may get into the nuances of the report; however, the SEC is generally just looking to see if there is a report or not.

The other primary rationale for a no-action letter is the "ordinary business"[69] rule, which is much more complex. In its simplest terms, just because you love jelly beans, a shareholder resolution asking that they be displayed by the checkout counters of all Walmart stores will be rejected through a no-action letter. Although that's fairly obvious, it turns out that the definition of "ordinary business" is a frequent source of debate.

For example, is it an infringement on a pharmacy chain's ordinary business if a shareholder resolution asks the company to disclose to shareholders the health impact of the tobacco products[70] it sells? Such a resolution may impose a burden on the chain's ability to sell the products that it wants to sell, so that would seem to be in the realm of "ordinary business." On the other hand, it seems to transcend day-to-day operations by dealing with the larger health impact of a product on consumers, which is a good argument to counter the claim of ordinary business. Isn't it reasonable for such a company to know—and to report to its shareholders—the risks of selling harmful products that may kill its customers?

Taking this idea a step further, what if a proposed shareholder resolution asked the company to disclose the effects of its candy sales, on the grounds that sugar is a major contributor to obesity and tooth decay? Is it reasonable to ask the pharmacy chain to disclose the impact of its sales of beer and wine, due to alcohol's obvious potential for abuse? Should it measure and report on the health effects of all scented products it sells because many people are allergic to perfume? What about selling firearms?

To a degree, the definition of "ordinary business" depends on who's doing the defining. In the text of a shareholder resolution, the inference of "ordinary business" may also rest on subtle nuances in the wording of the resolution. In any of the previous hypothetical examples, if the company objected to a resolution, claiming it pertained to ordinary business, it would take its concern to the SEC in the form of a no-action letter. You as a proponent would have the opportunity to make an opposing argument, and then the commission would give its opinion on the issue.

As discussed before, the SEC will likely support a corporation if a shareholder resolution pertains to a personal grievance. For example, just because your Internet provider's customer service rep was rude to you does not give you grounds to file a shareholder resolution asking the company to fire him. The company will challenge it. Also, another exclusion exists if the issue represents less than five percent of a company's revenue and assets and is not significantly related to the company's business. This is often hard to calculate for a big multinational if you are asking for a change related to one brand or product line, as the company may not break out this data.

HOW TO SUBMIT A DEFENDING BRIEF

If a company sends a no-action letter because it seeks to omit a resolution from the proxy ballot, the filer will receive a copy of the letter for review and have a chance to submit a defending brief to the SEC. Then SEC staff will have to make a decision, so the determination of what constitutes ordinary business is often a matter of interpretation based on previous case decisions. The arguments laid out in the no-action letter and defending brief are critical, so if possible, you should work with an attorney with experience defending proposals at the SEC. If you can't afford one, you can try writing the response yourself, especially if it's a fairly simple and straightforward argument. In the case of Alan Farago, described earlier, he simply tweaked his resolution and won, indicating that the company had a weak case but tried to block it regardless.

In 2015 As You Sow filed very similar Carbon Asset Risk resolutions with Chevron and ExxonMobil asking for "the Board of Directors to adopt and issue a dividend policy increasing the amount authorized for capital distribution to shareholders in light of the growing potential for stranded assets and decreasing profitability associated with capital expenditures on high cost, unconventional projects." Both companies challenged the filing. We defended as appropriate. The outcome was that the SEC supported ExxonMobil to omit the resolution and issued the opinion that Chevron could not omit, so only one of the two resolutions went to a vote. Unfortunately, the SEC decisions do not provide any rationale for why either decision was made.

CAN THE SEC DECISION BE CHALLENGED?

The SEC decision is only a recommendation advising the corporation that it is within its rights to omit the resolution from the proxy. However, the SEC ruling can be brought to a federal court where both parties can present their cases, and these decisions can then be appealed.

This happened in April 2015 where the 3rd US Circuit Court of Appeals vacated a permanent injunction imposed in November by US District Judge Leonard Stark that would have required a vote at Walmart's annual meeting in June of that year.[71]

This was a very high profile case where Walmart was asked by Trinity Church (the historic institution in the heart of Wall Street given its charter by King William III in 1697) to let shareholders vote on a proposal to tighten oversight of its sale of guns with high-capacity magazines.[72] Walmart had objected that allowing the Trinity Church proposal would "open the flood-gates" to more resolutions and cause interference in day-to-day business operations. The proposal asked Walmart's board to more closely examine the sale of products that might endanger public safety, hurt Walmart's reputation, or offend "family and commu-nity values" integral to brand.

Trinity's proposal argued that these products might include guns that enabled "mass killings in Newtown, Connecticut and Aurora, Colorado," with magazines holding more than 10 rounds. The resolution never made it to the proxy, but through the en-tire process, the public became very aware that Walmart's fam-ily values had been challenged. Because of the substantial costs involved in litigation, very few shareholders pursue a lawsuit to overturn an SEC decision.

HOW TO PROMOTE YOUR RESOLUTION

Assuming you either did not get a no-action letter or you won at the SEC, you can now turn your attention to get-out-the-vote strategies as even a low vote can have an impact if you can asso-ciate a brand with a specific issue.

If your resolution makes it to the proxy ballot, then the news media is a critical aid in gaining attention and support for your proposal. The goal, of course, is to get your point of view widely disseminated, and if you have the budget, you may want to hire a public relations agency to assist you.

The primary tool is the press release that has all of the essen-tial information about the initiative or event you are promoting. It's important to know that everyone in the news business—from newspaper reporters to business columnists to bloggers to web-site mavens—is busy. Consequently, a press release written in news style, thus requiring them to do little or no work, is more likely to be published by Reuters, wire services, and many bloggers. Major newspapers tend to take a release as a starting place. This is of great benefit to you, because it gets your point of view out to the public.

You can also blog and plunge into the social media melee, generating content on platforms like Twitter, Instagram, YouTube, and Facebook, which give your cause instantaneous global reach at no cost. You can also create an electronic press kit (EPK) so bloggers can grab an image or short summary of the story easily.

POSTING PROXY BRIEFINGS ON EDGAR[73]

Along with these promotional tools, there is another way that is more focused on the specific needs of investors. The same database that you may have used to look up shareholder resolutions, the Electronic Data Gathering Analysis and Retrieval system.[74] (EDGAR) performs automated collection, validation, indexing, acceptance, and forwarding of corporate submissions that are required by law and is freely available to the public via the Internet. Thanks to EDGAR, your shareholder resolution and any additional information you would like to file as part of an "exempt solicitation" or proxy memo will be available electronically for all shareholders to examine.

There is a fee based on word count to file this additional information, but using EDGAR gives you a chance to fully explain the rationale for your resolution and to include data, graphs, charts, links to other information online, and whatever other corroborating information you feel is important. Other than the fee for the word count, there is no word limit, so you can extoll the virtues of your resolution to your heart's content. The downside is that there's no interactivity or way to determine who's actually reading this material.

PROXY VOTING SERVICES AND INSTITUTIONAL SHAREHOLDERS

Institutions, foundations, philanthropic trusts, and investors who own a great variety of publically traded equities or who feel that they don't possess the time, tools, or expertise to vote their proxies appropriately can hire a proxy voting service to do it for them.

There are two major companies mentioned earlier that provide their services to vote your proxies, ISS (Institutional Shareholder Services) and Glass Lewis. Besides voting the shares of those they represent, the services evaluate and make voting recommendations on shareholder proposals, analyze issues, and maintain records of the votes. Many mutual funds, pension funds, and insurance funds vote according to the proxy services recommendations. If ISS endorses your shareholder resolution, you're likely to receive at least a ten percent favorable vote.

As mentioned before, the proxy voting services have guidelines on almost all issues, and although these firms overwhelmingly vote with management, they are open to being briefed on new issues, resolutions, and approaches outside of their published voting recommendations.

The vast majority of votes for proposals are often cast two weeks or more prior to the meeting, so it is important to ensure arguments for supporting your proposal are prepared at least one month in advance of the vote. As the sponsor of a shareholder resolution, you would contact, at minimum, both ISS and Glass Lewis. Beforehand, review their guidelines and tailor your presentation to address their historical concerns, because having them on your side can be an enormous help. If they decide to support your proposal, it is a major step forward in terms of your resolution being taken seriously by corporate management. Thus, your briefing for these proxy voting services is very important, and you should take the time to prepare thoroughly.

THE ANNUAL GENERAL MEETING

You or a representative must attend the AGM in order to "move," or present your resolution by reading a prepared statement. If you are a co-filer, the lead filer or their representative will be there, or if you happen to live in the city where the AGM is taking place, you may be asked to represent the group. It's a good idea to call the corporate secretary and ask in advance how much time you will have to speak. Three minutes is typical. Also, let them know who will be showing up on your behalf so they can expect you or one of your colleagues and check whether you'll need your verification of stock ownership, proxy letters, or other documentation. Just to be on the safe side, it's not a bad idea to bring them along. In addition, bring your personal identification, such as a driver's license.

The meeting may be in the corporate headquarters, a huge auditorium, a sports arena, a hotel conference room, or sometimes the restaurant of a country club. It may be attended by hundreds of people or only a handful of long-time shareholders and ex-employees. Whatever the setting or attendance, the AGM is a formal, scripted affair. In front of the attendees, the members of the board of directors will be seated in the front row or at a table. The corporate secretary will first welcome the audience and take care of SEC housekeeping. Next, the CEO usually gives a short talk about how the company is doing. Sometimes a video about the company is shown. In some rare cases, the first item of the day will be the proxy votes.

Proxy votes also proceed in a formal order. Voting to approve the auditors, board nominees, and executive compensation come first. Then, the shareholder resolutions are taken up. When your moment arrives, you are asked to go to the microphone, which is generally in an aisle facing the stage and podium. In some meetings, a security guard will hold the microphone. Most often, your time is kept informally; that is, if you speak too long, the CEO will ask you to wrap up. In other cases there is a countdown on the screen, and the microphone goes dead when time runs out.

Don't be late! Some meetings are very brief and can conclude within 15 minutes. If you are not present when called, the proposal will not have been legally presented for consideration, and the company is not obliged to release the vote total, which could negate all of your hard work.

Andy Warhol said that in the future, everyone will be famous for fifteen minutes. Speaking at a corporation's AGM may not really be equivalent to world fame, but this is your opportunity to directly address the management and the board, so make the most of it.

Proponents of shareholder resolutions typically read a prepared statement, which may or may not contain the actual text of
the resolution. Remember, your resolution has already been distributed, and the vast majority of voting will have already taken
place, too. Shareholders, or their representatives, will likely have
submitted their votes well ahead of the AGM.

Votes cast in advance can be changed as long as they meet
the stated deadlines—usually 24 hours before the meeting. Those
attending the annual meeting in person can change or submit
their votes up to the very last minute. When you take the microphone, it is your chance to put a human face to the cause you feel
so passionately about, and that's significant, as you are speaking
directly to the board and management of the company—the people who have the final decision regardless of the vote.

TALLYING THE VOTE

Proxy votes aren't like the returns on election night because
they are not simply Yes or No. Shareholders can vote either For,
Against, Abstain, or Not Voted. Shares that are not voted are automatically voted by management. This is why you always want to
vote your shares. If an investor is unsure about an issue, it is best
to abstain, as these votes are not cast for or against a resolution
and are not counted in the final legal tally.

The SEC calculates the Yes vote divided by Yes plus No votes
to determine if the resolution made the thresholds to be resubmitted (three percent the first year, six percent the second, and
10 percent in subsequent years.) Often at the AGM, the corporate secretary will do the math differently, making the vote seem
lower by adding the abstentions to the denominator. But within
four days of the AGM, the actual numbers must be publically
reported in what is called a form 8-K, and you will see the actual
counts and can check the calculations yourself.

Your shareholder resolution at Puppy, Inc. receives a very
respectable favorable vote of 25 percent, which is excellent. Although it is nonbinding and management and the board of directors is not obligated to institute the changes your resolution

suggested, if it ignores the resolution, it risks alienating one quarter of its shareholders, which it probably doesn't want to do.

Years ago, shareholder resolutions that achieved a 10 percent favorable vote were a rarity. But in the past couple of decades, as more shareholder advocates have gotten active and better at making their case and as shareholders generally have become accustomed to the process, favorable votes of 20 percent, 30 percent, and 40 percent have been achieved. That's a good thing. This means that shareholders are taking greater responsibility for the values that their investments represent and are no longer willing to silently let the status quo persist when it threatens those values.

However, even if you are carried out of the meeting on the shoulders of your supporters, flush with victory, now is the time to evaluate whether you have actually had an impact and made the change you desired. Often to truly implement and verify a transition takes tenacity and years of persistence.

THE COMMUNITY OF SHAREHOLDER ADVOCATES

Although you may have worked diligently and felt somewhat isolated, in fact you are part of a community of shareholder advocates working in a coalition and supporting each other. It is critically important to coordinate your efforts with this larger community especially as seeing the process through to make real change may take several years and require shifting tactics across filings at many companies.

That's why the majority of resolutions are submitted by professional organizations, such as socially responsible investing firms including (alphabetically) Arjuna Capital Management, Boston Common Asset Management, Calvert Investments, Christian Brothers Investments Services, Clean Yield Asset Management, Domini Social Investments, First Affirmative Financial Network, Green Century Capital Management, Harrington Investments, Jantz Management, Miller/Howard Investments, Newground Social Investment, Northstar Asset Management, Pax World Funds, Sonen Capital, Trillium Asset Management, Walden Asset Management, and Zevin Asset Management. Many corporate engagements leading to resolutions being filed are conducted by pension funds such as The California Public Employees' Retirement System (CalPERS), The California State Teachers' Retirement System (CalSTRS), New York City Public Pension Funds, New York State Common Retirement Fund, and the Connecticut Office of the State Treasurer as well as by nonprofits like The Humane Society, As You Sow, and SumOfUs, and foundations like the Nathan Cummings Foundation, the Christopher Reynolds Foundation, and the Needmor Fund. Organizations including Ceres and ICCR both coordinate filings; Ceres focuses mostly on climate and related environmental issues, while ICCR covers a much wider range of social and governance issues for their faith-based members. The most important take-away is that there is a robust community of shareholder advocates, and it is critical to coordinate your activities with them.

Your hypothetical shareholder resolution may not motivate a sudden about-face, and your appearance before the annual general meeting may not have been as galvanizing as Charlton Heston's appearance at Time Warner. However, an engagement that escalates to a well-crafted resolution is about putting forth a new idea. And ideas have power.

DRIVING CHANGE WITH NEW IDEAS

Nearly every major shareholder-driven corporate change started with a novel resolution. These resolutions push the envelope and can require time and investor education to resonate and build consensus; they highlight important areas of business risk and often see increased shareholder support in subsequent years, resulting in critical corporate changes that benefit both the corporation and shareholders. Also, the process of submitting shareholder resolutions is a critical part of expressing your rights as a shareholder and continues to expand in scope and importance.

Sometimes ideas like "Say on Pay,"[75] in which shareholders are empowered to vote on executive compensation packages every one, two, or three years, started as a shareholder resolution that was filed at enough companies, for enough years, with enough substantial votes that it became law. It is now required by the SEC under the Dodd-Frank Act. There are petitions at the SEC to consider other issues like disclosure of corporate lobbying and political spending to become a requirement for every company.

In fact, proxy access, which empowers long-term shareholders to nominate board candidates for the proxy ballot, was set to become an SEC rule for all public companies in 2010. The Chamber of Commerce challenged it in court and won,[76] so it was not implemented as a rule for all public companies. Instead, shareholders, led by the New York City Pension Funds, brought it forth as a resolution at hundreds of companies and had it voted on. After one year, it has already been adopted by and is in the by-laws of over 70 companies, and it looks like it may spread to all public companies soon.

The power of an individual shareholder is to bring forth new ideas. However, it often takes building a coalition to change a company and an industry. A recent example of this is the idea of stranded carbon assets. This concept was first introduced by the Carbon Tracker Initiative in their seminal 2011 Carbon Bubble report.[77] It was used as the foundation of a shareholder resolution filed in 2012 for the first time by As You Sow at CONSOL Energy.[78] Simultaneously, Ceres organized 70 investment entities with $3 trillion of assets under management to sign a letter to 45 of the world's top oil, gas, coal, and electric power companies.[79]

This led to 11 companies receiving similar resolutions the next year from a coalition of faith-based, pension, SRI, and nonprofit shareholder advocates. As You Sow's work led ExxonMobil to agree to prepare the first report by a major oil company in response to investor concerns about climate asset risk. The concept of stranded assets was one of the main drivers at the Paris COP 21 climate talks. It has been adopted by The Bank of England and major reinsurers and is a fundamental concept underlying a global coalition on climate finance analyzing the risks of climate change and the transition to a clean energy future.

Filing shareholder resolutions is part of the ecosystem of change, and as long as you are transparent and communicate your intention to other advocates working in the space, you will be welcomed to play a part.

8

What Kind of People Engage with Corporations?

M any activists came of age in the 1960s, first with the civil rights movement and then with protests against the Vietnam War. Watch any episode of *Mad Men* to get a taste of the stifling social and political structure of the period, and you'll understand why a rejection of authority was also a component of the protest period. If you are a millennial, you may have seen a movie set in that time when expressions like "Never trust anyone over 30" were common. In the wake of the civil rights and anti-Vietnam war movements, the focus then turned to what became the environmental movement with the publication of Rachel Carson's pioneering *Silent Spring*[80] in 1962 and the first Earth Day in 1970.[81] For many, distrust of authority came along with these movements.

Distrust of the establishment isn't misplaced. Many giant corporations are not instruments of social good. They are instruments of profit. In the past several decades, with the escalating globalization of the economy, corporations have grown far more powerful and far more remote from the concerns of ordinary people. The pressure for short-term profits drives decisions to externalize their pollution at no cost to companies' bottom lines but at a huge cost to society at large.

However, to negotiate with them, to learn about how they think, to speak their language, and to find common ground does not mean that you have succumbed to their values or compromised your own. It represents, instead, a recognition of reality: while we may not like it, large corporations do exist, and it's not likely that they'll disappear any time soon. After all, they wield an enormous—and increasing—amount of power. As shareholders, you are part of this power structure. To engage with companies is to direct some of that power toward creating sustainable businesses that benefit not only shareholders but also the world in which they operate.

SAY IT AIN'T SO, JOE

It goes without saying that a chorus requires more than one voice, so allying yourself with an existing community of like-minded people has obvious advantages. For years, churches and faith-based organizations have been very active in issues of social justice, and those issues have often touched upon corporate behavior. It was through his religious order that Reverend Michael Crosby took on the tobacco industry starting in the 1970s.

Reverend Crosby probably doesn't fit the expected profile of a shareholder advocate. He's a Catholic priest at the Province of St. Joseph of the Capuchin Order. In the late 1970s, Crosby was visiting Nicaragua, where his order had a mission, and he couldn't help but notice how the countryside was plastered with billboards extolling the glories of the revolution and its leader, Daniel Ortega. "I had kind of a distinct reaction," Crosby said. "How can people be so influenced by such propaganda?"

Soon after his visit to Nicaragua, Crosby was at another mission in Costa Rica. The road to the airport there was lined with billboards, too, but these were quite different. "One billboard after another advertised this and that, and a huge number were cigarettes," said Crosby, a recovering three-pack-a-day smoker.

The billboards in both countries touted different things, but the campaigns were similar. "All of a sudden it hit me that both were propaganda. In the United States and throughout the world in the market economy, it's 'buy, buy, buy.' What is the difference between one revolution and the other?"

Crosby decided to start something of a revolution of his own. When he returned to the United States, he asked his treasurer to buy ten shares of R.J. Reynolds Tobacco and ten shares of Philip Morris. The small ownership stake was enough to give the order standing to attend the corporations' next annual general meetings and to file shareholder resolutions if necessary.

When he studied the demographics of smoking, it became clear to Crosby that the majority of smokers begin the habit when they were in their teenage years—just as he had. Father Crosby refined his focus and efforts on addressing the impact that cigarette advertising had on young people.

The Marlboro Man, the peppy models for Virginia Slims with their slogan "You've come a long way, baby," and the defiant Tareyton smokers who would rather fight than switch, were arguably created by Madison Avenue "Mad Men" in the 1960s to appeal to adults.

But what about Joe Camel, the lovable cartoon dromedary who touted R.J. Reynolds's Camel brand in magazine and billboard ads? Created in 1974 and first used in French ad campaigns, Joe Camel appeared in the United States starting in 1988. Although he lacked a hump, Joe Camel had attitude to spare, and he had lots of leisure time, too. He rode a motorcycle, played pool, and hung out in a hot tub with bikini-clad babes. In short, he did everything an adolescent boy longed to do. Oh, and a Camel cigarette always dangled from his lip.

Talk about swagger. Did he have a face that could pretty easily be confused with parts of the male anatomy? Would advertisers stoop so low? It's a matter of debate. Google "Joe Camel images" (as we could not get the rights to publish a picture of Joe in this book), and you decide.

Of course, only a cynic would suggest that Joe Camel's mission was to recruit younger smokers to take the place of the ones dying by the thousands of lung cancer and emphysema.

Crosby focused particularly on R.J. Reynolds, and unfortunately for them, the barrage of publicity, lawsuits, and the shareholder resolution brought by Crosby's group and by others brought a lot of attention to the matter of youth smoking, including a

1991 study in the *Journal of the American Medical Association* that showed that as many six-year-olds knew that Joe Camel was linked to tobacco as knew that Mickey Mouse was tied to Disney.

R.J. Reynolds doesn't inspire the same affection as Disney, and Crosby had it out for Joe Camel, just as he would for a drug dealer hanging around the candy store.

"We generated a tremendous amount of publicity about Joe Camel and its appeal to youth," said Crosby. "Ultimately, we were one of the voices that got Reynolds to stop. Then we found out they were doing it abroad, and so we filed shareholder actions internationally, and they stopped. That was a big campaign with a significant result."

Crosby's campaign against the detrimental health effects of tobacco continues to the present day and has included shareholder resolutions, negotiations, public demonstrations, legal action, political lobbying, and more.

Crosby's engagement with tobacco companies brought other issues to Crosby's attention. "About ten years ago . . . I happened to be giving a retreat to some nuns in Louisville and learned about some migrant workers who got green tobacco sickness (acute nicotine poisoning). It comes when you touch the leaf in the morning, when there is dew on the leaf. It won't kill you, but it sure gives you a rough time; there is vomiting, nausea, and it's very, very painful. So I filed a resolution on that, and Louis C. Camilleri, the president of Phillip Morris, said he never had heard of it."

Crosby was stunned by the revelation. "Here this priest is telling a company whose whole business is around tobacco procurement about a huge problem connected with labor's harvesting of the product, and he said on the record that he'd never heard of it."

The field workers knew about it, and until Crosby came along, no one had given them a voice. At least, no one had given them a voice loud enough to be heard in the board room. Fueled by a desire to address green tobacco illness among field laborers, Crosby's order has gone on to file numerous resolutions on the issue of green tobacco sickness, human rights, and the exploitation of workers. It turns out there's a strong association between youth viewing characters in movies who smoke and their own initiation of smoking. So Crosby and ICCR, along with As You Sow, initiated a shareholder engagement o get Hollywood studios to reduce risk to their brand by removing smoking from youthrated movies. Companies were encouraged to pressure the Motion Picture Association of America (MPAA) to require an "R" rating for all movies with smoking imagery—a practice that would save 1,000,000 lives, according to a 2012 Surgeon General report and backed up with CDC data.[82]

A "MINOW" SWIMMING WITH SHARKS

The Occupy movement, commencing in New York's Zuccotti Park on September 17, 2011,[83] focused the nation's attention on income inequality and brought into the lexicon a new and potent phrase, "the one percent," which became shorthand for all manner of corporate greed and excess.

Fighting that battle on the inside has been Nell Minow, known as "Movie Mom"[84] on beliefnet.com for reviewing films with a kid-friendly eye. So it's no surprise that film references often find their way into her observations about corporate governance. "Have you seen *The Solid Gold Cadillac?*" she asked. Produced in 1956, the film stars Judy Holiday as a minority stockholder who takes on a crooked board of directors at a corporate annual meeting. "The CEO in the film earns a whopping $150,000 per year," Minow said. "Just add three zeroes to that, and, really, nothing has changed."

Nell also is very concerned with corporate governance and has been working on this issue for decades as the editor of The Corporate Library, an independent research firm that rates boards of directors of public companies and compiles research, study, and critical thinking about corporate governance.

Her business partner Robert Monks was a founder of Institutional Shareholder Services (ISS), which provides governance research, data, and recommendations as well as various proxy and securities services. Minow joined him in that firm and then in two others. She credits her business partner with inventing the idea of the proxy adviser. "His great insight was that there was a massive collective choice problem that was preventing effective shareholder engagement," Minow said.

ELEVATOR PITCH

In the early nineties, Minow and Monks started the Lens Fund, a $100 million investment firm dedicated to shareholder activism. Their objective was to buy stock in underperforming companies and use various shareholder initiatives to try to get them to improve their environmental, social, and governance policies. The first real initiative involved Sears, where Monks ran for a seat on the board. Sears responded to Monk's bid by shrinking the size of the board, which made his election mathematically impossible. At the time Sears had several divisions: the stores, which were the worst performing of the various parts of the company, but also an insurance company, a real estate company, and other units.

It was Minow's objective to get the company to break out the individual operations. "I think my favorite moment in the history of my life in corporate governance was when Bob went to a meeting with the CEO of Sears in what was then the Sears Tower," Minow recalled. "The CFO came to meet him in the lobby and they rode up in the elevator together, just the two of them." At the time, the Sears Tower was the tallest building in the world, so the pair had several minutes "just standing there listening to the Muzak as they're going up and up and up to the 78th floor," Minow said. As they climbed higher, the CFO turned to Monks. "This is the first time bad news has gone above the 72nd floor," he quipped.

To Minow, that remark "is corporate governance in a nutshell. You want to make sure the bad news gets up to the 78th floor."

Their demand that the board break up the company into its constituent parts grew heated, to the extent that Minow took dramatic and public action: taking out a full-page ad in the *Wall Street Journal*, calling the Sears board of directors "non-performing assets" and publishing all their names in the ad. Those names included Donald Rumsfeld, who later was Secretary of Defense. The ad has become legendary in the annals of corporate governance advocacy. The company was eventually broken up.

Minow may swim with sharks, but she isn't afraid of them and is devoted to making corporate boards more responsive and more accountable to shareholders. Her particular targets are the boards of poorly governed corporations. One board of directors that got into the crosshairs of Minow and Monks was Stone & Webster, a large engineering and construction firm. How badly was it governed? "It was trading at under the value of its real estate," Minow said.

Minow is renowned for her blunt assessments. In the case of Stone & Webster, she said, "You could have shut it

Figure 7: This 1992 full-page ad in the Wall Street Journal brought governance issues at Sears into stark focus and proposed ways to reinvigorate the company's sinking reputation, urging stockholders to vote in favor of shareholder proposals.

Used with permission of Nell Minow and Bob Monks.

down, told everyone to go home, and just sold the real estate, and you would get your money back. That's what a disaster it was." The company had used accounting tricks to make it look profitable: thanks to a booming stock market, the company's pension fund had a surplus, which was improperly combined with earnings.

From Minow's point of view, blame for the company's moribund performance fell squarely on the shoulders of its board of directors. She was determined to do something about it. Minow and Monks attended Stone & Webster's annual meeting on behalf of clients. They were among perhaps a total of 25 people at the event. Early on, the Chairman announced that they had a busy agenda and would cap shareholder comments to three minutes.

Monks objected. "I'm sorry," he said. "Do you have someplace else you have to be?"

The time limit was dismissed.

Routine business was quickly dispatched, and then it was time for the election of directors. If Minow hadn't been there, the election would have been done in moments, she said. But she had a question: "I'm trying to decide whether I want to vote for these directors or not, so I would like each of them to get up and explain to all of us here why the stock of this company is a bad investment."

The Board was flabbergasted by the question. "Well, what do you mean it's a bad investment?"

"Well, we've got five million dollars' worth of stock on behalf of our clients, and nobody on the board has more than 200 shares, so if you don't think it is a good place for your money, what am I missing?"

One of the directors said, "I make it a policy never to discuss my personal investments."

Minow was ready for her. "According to Forbes you are a billionaire, so you can afford to invest more. You've been on the board of this company for ten years; you have 100 shares. I'm going to come back every year until you buy some stock."

Another board member said, "I'm Canadian and it is very complicated for me to have property in the United States."

"That's just not a good answer," Minow said, and then assured him that there were lawyers who could help him.

GETTING TO NO

Minow has focused on corporate governance because in her view it encompasses everything else. "You can't get anywhere on any other issue without addressing the issue of the board," she said. "The more I do this, the more I realize that the only thing that really matters is who is on the board."

It would seem like dissatisfied shareholders could simply promote board candidates of their own, but Minow hasn't found that to be an effective course. Finding qualified candidates who wish to run is "brutal" because they know that, if elected, they'll struggle for credibility and probably find their initiatives stonewalled by the other more orthodox members. Minow strongly favors voting ineffective members off the board as a sign of shareholder discontent. Getting a "no" vote against a sitting board member sends a powerful signal.

THAR SHE BLOWS

A great example of the power of shareholders to vote no and send a no-confidence vote to a board member occurred at JP Morgan after the infamous "London Whale"[85] incident. It's important to remember that shareholder resolutions are a level of escalation in your engagement with a corporation. The first step is always communication: letters on behalf of shareholders stating a given concern and laying out a viable solution.

One hopes that rationality and logic are powerful enough, but often that's not the case. Perhaps that's because corporations and shareholder advocates speak a different language. But even when the same language is spoken, sometimes change can be difficult to bring about. After the global financial collapse of 2008, you would think that the message would be clear in any language: stop sweeping risky investments under the rug!

It appeared, to some at least, that JP Morgan Chase—which survived the 2008 financial meltdown—had gotten that message. In 2012 it was earning billions in profit under CEO and Chairman Jamie Dimon. At that time, Bruno Iksil, a trader in the London office, initiated a series of complex derivative trades[86]—the same financial instruments that earned such a nasty reputation in 2008. Iskil's trades lost the bank a whopping $6.2 billion and earned Iskil the nickname "The London Whale" when it came to light that he and his colleagues were keeping two sets of books to hide the losses.

Of course, the loss came as a complete surprise to everyone. Well, not exactly. As early as 2008, according to a 2014 report by the Federal Reserve's Inspector General, examiners at the New York Federal Reserve Bank had spotted risks in the unit's trading practices. They just didn't follow up.

As the London Whale debacle unfolded, enter Bill Patterson, executive director of the CtW Investment Group. Founded in 2006, CtW works with pension funds sponsored by unions affiliated with Change to Win, a federation of unions representing nearly 5.5 million members. Before establishing CtW, Patterson—in the investment field since the 1980s—was one of the first to shine a spotlight on Enron before its 2001 bankruptcy.

With CtW, he continued his mission to enhance shareholder value through active management of the investments held by its members. "We went after the banks, including JP Morgan Chase because they weren't managing their subprime risk," he said. "We sent letters to six of the big banks and met with the board directors and the six committees."

The reforms he recommended were largely dismissed. Three of those banks no longer exist. Among the survivors was JP Morgan Chase. But its survival wasn't due to exemplary management. For years, Patterson had been clamoring for changes but had gotten little support from shareholders. According to Patterson, "they supported no independent proposals and reflexively voted for the board." One of the problems with that was that the board of directors had essentially become an echo chamber for Jamie Dimon. But after the London Whale breached the surface, it was obvious that something was wrong.

It was Patterson's view that the risk management committee not only lacked checks and balances but "was not on top of what was required to manage risk." The London Whale only made that more obvious, especially the aftermath, when "there was a new wave of revelations about misconduct that confirmed our contention," Patterson said.

Of the greatest concern to Patterson were the apparent conflicts of interest of a board member who sat on the risk management committee. Ellen Futter, according to Patterson, lacked any risk management experience at all. "She was president of the Natural History Museum in New York," he said. JP Morgan CEO Jamie Dimon was also on the Natural History Museum's board, and JP Morgan Chase donated money to the museum.

To Patterson, the conflict of interest was clear. "It just seemed like [Futter] was an inappropriate director for that committee," said Patterson.

But how do you get rid of a member of the board who isn't right for the job? "You talk to the company," Patterson said. "You begin with diplomacy, and if that doesn't work, then you escalate." Getting changes in the board is often a behind-the-scenes campaign of letter writing and persuading other shareholders to withhold support for ineffective board members, and to vote against their pay packages in annual proxy votes.

Patterson and others worked hard to garner support among shareholders to withhold support, and when the vote came, Ellen Futter resigned.

USING SUPPLY CHAINS TO STOP THE CHAIN SAWS

Corporations have enormous resources and whole departments—along with advertising and public relations agencies—devoted to burnishing their brand image. They can bring these to bear against you, or you can turn those forces in your favor. That's what happened in the battle to stop Home Depot from selling old-growth lumber.

Starting in the mid-1980s there had been years of confrontations between environmental activists and logging companies to stop the clear-cutting of old-growth rainforests[87] at locations around the world and, in particular, British Columbia's Clayoquot Sound ancient forest and at the Headwaters redwood forest in Humboldt County, California.

Dozens of organizations were involved, including Friends of Clayoquot Sound,[88] Bay Area Coalition for Headwaters (BACH),[89] Environment Protection Information Center (EPIC),[90] Trees Foundation,[91] Sierra Club,[92] Rainforest Action Network,[93] Greenpeace,[94] Rose Foundation,[95] and many others.

The battles involved tree sits, including the epic 738 days in a Redwood named Luna by Julia Butterfly Hill,[96] as well as legal actions, protests, banner hangs, boycotts, acts of civil disobedience, political intervention, and congressional action. In 1996 activist groups turned their attention on companies that were purchasing old-growth lumber to try and stop the demand in the supply chain.

Thomas Van Dyck saw an opportunity to add the power of shareholder advocacy to the mix. Looking down the supply chain of MacMillan Bloedel, Canada's largest lumber company that was clear-cutting pristine coastal rain forests, he decided to focus on one of their largest customers, Pacific Telesis Group (PacTel), the landline phone service provider for Northern California. They were grinding up the old-growth wood for phone books, "The trade-off appeared increasingly absurd—would shareholders want the company brand associated with ancient forests being destroyed for phone books that were thrown away after one year? There was business risk here." So, he decided to file a shareholder resolution.

Previous attempts to pressure companies that directly owned the forests had been difficult—this was their primary source of revenue. But PacTel didn't own the forests; they could easily shift to a sustainable paper supplier for their phone books. The resolution earned an 8.9 percent vote, sent a message, and brought public scrutiny to the issue.

Next up on the supply chain was Home Depot. Rainforest Action Network had been organizing protests at the stores, and it occurred to Tom that shareholders were losing brand value every day. He asked one of his clients, Educational Foundation of America, that owned Home Depot shares to complement their grant making and their mission by authorizing the filing of a shareholder resolution. Thomas then hired Michael Passoff, a University of Alberta PhD student who had left his research on the Clayoquot Sound rainforests to join the fight to stop clear-cut logging in 1993. Michael, working with Conrad MacKerron and allies at Trillium Asset Management, filed the resolution and engaged in dialogue asking Home Depot to write a report on phasing out sales of old-growth wood.

Intensive negotiations did not bring about an agreement to withdraw the resolution, so it went to a vote at the company's 1999 annual general meeting. At the time, most resolutions were struggling to get a five percent favorable vote, making anything higher than that significant. Thomas, Conrad, and Michael adopted a tactic rarely used before on environmental or social resolutions, launching a large-scale solicitation and get-out-the-proxy-vote campaign to gain investor support. They developed an investor fact sheet that highlighted the reputational and financial risks of using old-growth wood as well as the benefits of using available alternatives, such as wood certified by the Forest Stewardship Council.[97] The financial arguments supporting the resolution were mailed to the company's top 5,000 investors, and they personally called the top 150 shareholders to provide additional details.

The resolution received the support of 113 million shares or 11.8 percent—one of the highest environmental resolution votes of that year. The high approval rate got the attention of *Wall Street Journal*, *The New York Times*, the *San Francisco Chronicle*, and other major media. Press coverage at this level put pressure on Home Depot to act and aroused public interest, increasing the

> **FOREST STEWARDSHIP COUNCIL** After the 1992 Earth Summit in Rio failed to produce an agreement to stop deforestation, a group of businesses, environmentalists, and community leaders came together to create the Forest Stewardship Council (FSC).Gathered in the first FSC General Assembly in 1993 in Toronto, Canada, the group set out to create a voluntary, market-based approach that would improve forest practices worldwide. Today, FSC operates in more than 80 countries, and has certified 187 million hectares to best-practice criteria.

likelihood that if Home Depot did nothing, more shareholder resolutions would be filed in upcoming years, more customers would take their business elsewhere, more demonstrators would appear, and more damage would be done to the Home Depot brand.

Three months later Home Depot agreed to phase out sales of old-growth wood by 2002. The company released a wood purchasing policy that stated it "will give preference to the purchase of wood and wood products originating from certified well-managed forests." They committed to eliminating wood purchases from "endangered regions around the world" and to promoting the use of "alternative environmental products."

Yet the company's ensuing lack of communication led shareholders to refile the resolution in 2000. According to Passoff, "We had a hard decision to make. The dialogue had stalled although we knew they were making progress in searching for certified wood and working with World Wildlife Fund, Natural Resources Defense Council, and others to identify endangered forests. But the action plan on developing a tracking system and identifying alternative suppliers was well behind schedule. We flew to Atlanta to meet with them, and they updated us on the challenges they were facing in developing new processes. They shared their supplier questionnaire with us for feedback, and overall we felt that things were moving, although taking longer than promised."

This is an example of how company dialogues are complex, and there is a give and take, trust earned and trust broken, and ultimately the time clock on real progress is ticking. Bottom line, the resolution was withdrawn. Meanwhile, Rainforest Action Network (RAN) continued, and even escalated their protests. According to *Time* magazine, the week of June 24, 2001 RAN staged a day of action in 70 cities,[98] according to former RAN Executive Director and founder Randy Hayes, "Customers will be offered 'rain forest tours' through the store, spotlighting products made with trees from pristine, old-growth forests around the world: dowels and tool handles of ramin wood from Southeast Asia, doors of Amazon mahogany, cedar shingles, Douglas fir lumber from the temperate rain forests of North America, and lauan plywood from the Philippines and Indonesia."

As You Sow and Trillium Asset Management's engagement continued, and by year-end 2002 Home Depot was another step closer to making good on its commitment to eliminate the purchase of wood and wood products from endangered regions around the world. They were promoting certification under the Forest Stewardship Council standards. They worked to develop definitions to translate "old-growth" into industry terms that had meaning to loggers and encouraged more responsible forestry practices in several hot spots, including Indonesia and the Central Coast of British Columbia.

By 2003, Home Depot was still not 100 percent old-growth wood–free but had become the industry leader in promoting responsible wood purchases. In shareholder dialogue the company said they were thankful, saying that even though it took three years, they could now source wood "from store to stump," and the overall process improved their tracking system and resilience of their supply chain encompassing 5,000 suppliers and over 50,000 products.

GET THE LEAD DOG AND THE PACK FOLLOWS

The work by Home Depot paid unexpected benefits, because as soon as they had seen the light, their major competitor, Lowe's, knew it looked bad in comparison. Lowe's wanted to match Home Depot's policies. Whatever its motives—environmental responsibility, raw competitiveness, or fear that their company would be in the crosshairs next—wasn't all that important. Then it was like dominos, on down the line with the different wood products retailers all signing up.

Home Depot had been chosen for many reasons, chief among them that it was a market leader, and as a consequence several other major industry players with combined wood sales of nearly $20 billion followed, but change might have been much slower if the press coverage had not linked the fight to their logo. As was mentioned earlier, a brand's value is estimated at 27 percent[99] of the company market capitalization. For Home Depot that meant over $6 billion dollars in value that management was fighting to keep.

After Home Depot agreed to phase out sale of old-growth wood products and give preference to FSC certified wood, Office

Depot received shareholder resolutions and soon agreed to an internal ban on paper sourced from old-growth forests and increased their stock of office paper with 30 percent post-consumer waste content. Following suit, Staples committed to sell 30 percent average post-consumer waste content paper and cease sourcing from endangered forests in 2002 after shareholder dialogue, a resolution, and a grassroots campaign led by environmental groups. Both later agreed to sell 100 percent recycled paper.

The whole point of the engagement with the retailers was to impact the supply chain leading back to the chain saws in the forest.

BRAND REPUTATION AS A LEVER FOR CHANGE

Corporations go to a lot of expense burnishing their reputation and building their brand's public image, as it is incredibly valuable. Coca Cola doesn't sell soft drinks; they sell a "brand." Consequently, as the Home Depot example shows, companies are skittish if that brand's image is threatened. Imagine how the giant Swiss food and beverage company Nestlé felt in the 1970s when it was labeled a "baby killer." At the time Nestlé was heavily promoting infant formula as a superior alternative to breast milk in developing countries. Nursing mothers with little education and less experience evaluating the veracity of marketing campaigns believed the hype.

Once mothers stopped nursing their babies, their breast milk dried up, of course, and mothers had no choice but to continue using formula. The stuff was very expensive for average households, so many mothers watered it down—using contaminated water in some cases—to make it go further.

Healthcare experts and critics said the resulting malnutrition, along with the transmission of water-borne illnesses, led to sickness and the deaths of many infants. This was labelled "commercially caused malnutrition." Then, in March 1974, a booklet by Mike Muller and published by "War on Want" detailing the campaign and provocatively titled *The Baby Killer*[100] was published in

Britain. Although Nestlé sued, the Baby Killer label stuck and soon aroused what would become a multinational global boycott of Nestlé products. So, the "outside" component was in high gear.

THE FAITH-BASED SHAREHOLDER COMMUNITY WEIGHS IN

These actions were complemented by a shareholder strategy, too. This was coordinated by the Interfaith Center on Corporate Responsibility (ICCR), whose executive director was Tim Smith. ICCR was composed of a number of Protestant and Roman Catholic investors. Infant formula abuse soon became one of its top priorities.

Together, they filed shareholder resolutions with US formula manufacturers to halt the heavy promotion of bottle feeding over nursing. As those shareholder resolutions grew, ICCR continued playing a prominent role in the campaign, which included a court suit against Bristol Myers by ICCR member the Sisters of the Precious Blood and ultimately blossomed into a worldwide boycott of Nestlé. Eventually, the World Health Organization and UNICEF stepped forward, establishing an international code of conduct for companies making and selling baby formula.

The companies begrudgingly accepted the standards, and after a couple of years, the sky had not fallen. In fact, Tim Smith said that, on balance, this campaign

Figure 7A: Published in 1974, The Baby Killer booklet informed a global campaign that is still associated with the Nestlé brand. *Used with permission of War on Want.*

was probably good for the companies. They got a chance to meet some of their critics and investors, and the changes advocated led to better business practices and a more favorable public image, among other things.

Maybe if Nestlé had simply listened to the public health community and investors at the start and paid closer attention to what was happening on the ground with its products, they could have prevented a lot of damage to their brand and, most importantly, prevented many senseless deaths.

ACTION GUIDED BY FAITH

Sister Nora Nash's life of shareholder advocacy is profoundly influenced by her faith. A member of ICCR and the Philadelphia Coalition for Responsible Investment, Nash is a sister of St. Francis of Philadelphia, and serves as the Director of Corporate Social Responsibility for her congregation. Attending a country school in Limerick, Ireland, Nash said, "We were always involved in doing something for the foreign missions and helping those who were poor. That was a very important part of my childhood. We were not rich, and we were not really poor, but we knew there were people worse off than ourselves."

Community outreach was an important part of her ministry as an educator, working with students and parents to provide meals and clothing for those who were homeless, and delivering hundreds of Thanksgiving baskets to the less fortunate. "That part of social justice was always part of my life, and it is also part of our mission as Franciscans."

While teaching junior high students in the 1970s, Nash was active at a local level in a campaign to stop the clothing manufacturer Farah from using sweatshop labor in Texas, and her life as an advocate for corporate responsibility has only grown since then. Among the most significant campaigns Nash has been involved with were those against predatory credit card company lending practices and predatory loans, including opaque lending agreements and the targeting of students, which led to enactment of the Credit Card Act in 2009.

This federal statute was passed by the United States Congress and signed by President Barack Obama on May 22, 2009. It is comprehensive credit card reform legislation that aims "to establish fair and transparent practices relating to the extension of credit under an open end consumer credit plan, and for other purposes."

Then, and to the present day, Nash and others in her order are active in issues "that challenge our society, whether it is human rights, fracking, climate change, trafficking, or ministering to and with those who are disenfranchised." Her commitment goes well beyond the economic realm. "We have a commitment to living our mission which is to live 'the passion of the Gospel' as St. Francis did, and 'take the necessary risks to be a healing, compassionate presence in our violent world.'"

9

Foundations and Individual Shareholders Can Make a Difference

In 1993, Steve Viederman, then heading up the Jessie Smith Noyes Foundation, noticed that the foundation's portfolio included stock with Intel. Viederman knew that one of the Noyes Foundation's grantees, the Southwest Organizing Project (SWOP), had been trying to get information on Intel's environmental emissions and water usage in New Mexico. The foundation gave a grant to SWOP so it could become a shareholder, and it used its shares to begin a shareholder dialog with the company. The first year, the shareholder resolution got seven percent of the vote, which allowed Noyes to commit to filing a second year. But before that happened, the company responded and gave SWOP the information it sought. Viederman was an early leader in the foundation community, understanding how to combine shareholder and grassroots power.

In 2007, the *Los Angeles Times*[101] published a blistering investigative story showing how some of the investments of the Bill and Melinda Gates Foundation were increasing social problems that the foundation's programs sought to combat. The *Times* found that the foundation had invested $400 million in oil companies like Royal Dutch Shell, ExxonMobil, and Chevron, which were responsible for flares blanketing the Niger Delta with pollution, causing an epidemic of bronchitis, asthma, and blurred vision in children at the same time the foundation was spending millions of dollars to improve health in the area.

The story reinvigorated the debate within the philanthropic and grantee community about whether and how foundations and their grantees should use their assets and investments to boost their philanthropic missions and partner with those they fund to organize for change. Gates Foundation CEO Patty Stonecipher said that changes in foundation investment practices would have little or no impact on social or environmental issues. Sadly, that view failed to recognize a decade of documented success with foundations supporting shareholder advocacy with organizations they fund and support, adding vision and strategy.

Another example of a highly active foundation using shareholder advocacy to advance its mission while integrating Environment, Social, and Governance (ESG) criteria across their entire investment portfolio has been the Educational Foundation of America (EFA). The foundation had long sought to promote environmental resource efficiency in its grant programs, funding activist groups on responsible forestry practices, recycling, and recycled content. The foundation realized it could use its position as an investor in major companies to press for positive change as well. EFA's investment consultant was Thomas Van Dyck. According to John Powers, EFA board member, "Our portfolio was fully aligned with our mission and was outperforming. Engaging companies in shareholder action to complement our grant-making was a natural next step for us." In 1995, EFA began a long partnership with As You Sow that resulted in a string of significant victories in the area of recycling and resource efficiency.

EFA's board decided to leverage the 95 percent of its assets to improve the environmental performance of companies in its investment portfolio. "Foundations were created under the IRS tax code to leverage social change," Powers said, "Every tool available to them should be used."

As You Sow went to work using a strategy of developing shareholder initiatives on companies held in EFA's investment portfolio, which, because they passed the foundation's ESG investment screens, potentially made them more open to dialogue about improving their environmental performance. Noting the poor recycling rate for beverage bottles and cans, As You Sow program director Conrad MacKerron engaged Coca-Cola Co. to set take-back and recycled content goals for its bottles and cans. He assembled a coalition of ESG investor groups, and following several years of dialogue and shareholder votes, the company agreed to take actions that would result in collection and recycling of the equivalent of 50 percent of its bottles and cans by the end of 2015. This included a $50 million investment in what was at the time the world's largest recycling plant for the plastic known as polyethylene terephthalate (PET) found in the hundreds of millions of beverage bottles sold every day. Working with Boston SRI firm Walden Asset Management, As You Sow later received a similar commitment from PepsiCo, to recycle 60 percent of industry bottles and cans by 2018.

EFA shares were used in successful efforts pressing Staples and Office Depot to use higher levels of recycled content in office paper sold under their names. EFA was engaged in the As You Sow effort to have Best Buy, the largest US electronics retailer, agree to an unprecedented free electronics take-back program in all 1,000 US stores starting in 2007. Because Best Buy agreed on the idea after an initial dialogue, there was no need to file a shareholder resolution. The Best Buy take-back program has been a huge success and has already recovered one billion pounds of electronics with a new goal of two billion by 2020. It is also a profit center for the company. EFA was also in partnership on successful actions by As You Sow engaging Home Depot and allies to stop selling old-growth timber and Apple Inc. to triple its electronic waste take-back programs.

Why so much success? One factor is that companies like those engaged on behalf of EFA had already passed ESG investor screens. Within such companies, corporate management is often already attuned to corporate stewardship and has incorporated sustainability goals to the point that proposals suggesting improvement are greeted more often with reasoned consideration than reflexive opposition.

Companies are often savvy enough to see how a proposed action can be a win-win-win situation by solving an environmental problem, improving customer service, and boosting sales all at the same time. In the Best Buy example cited on e-waste recycling, the company correctly surmised that by offering a convenient way for customers to drop off old computers, TVs, and cell phones, it could not just keep these materials out of landfills but also provide customers a welcome way to clean out their closets of old electronics, and drive traffic to its stores, where many stayed and shopped.

The EFA experience shows how foundations can exponentially increase the value of their program work by simultaneously funding shareholder advocacy actions in the same program areas. EFA's actions helped lead to recycling of 20 billion bottles and cans and 500,000 tons of e-waste per year. "EFA has been a leader on so many shareholder campaigns that have made a difference," Thomas Van Dyck said. "They came to understand the tool and to use it to create significant change.

SOMETIMES IT TAKES TENACITY

Shareholder advocates often work with multiple organizations to bring about change and broaden the platform by which a given issue can gain greater public attention. A good example is a series of shareholder resolutions filed by As You Sow on behalf of investor Cari Rudd, who later joined the board.

We met Cari through a mutual acquaintance, Lisa Renstrom, who had authorized us to file a shareholder resolution with Duke Energy on the risks of storing coal ash near their power plants. Cari and Lisa both belonged to Rachel's Network,[102] an environmental organization named after the author Rachel Carson, the scientist and environmental advocate who in 1962 wrote the groundbreaking book *Silent Spring* about the impact of the indiscriminate use of pesticides on the environment generally and bird populations specifically.

Cari was interested in our use of corporate engagement to bring about positive change. Rudd, a long-time environmental activist and former board chair of the Environmental Working Group, had a long history of successful advocacy for environmental and political campaigns and was an experienced investor.

For some time, we had been in dialog with Abbott Laboratories, asking them to bring a non-GMO version of their popular infant formula, Similac, to market in the United States. Even though they produced and sold it in Europe, where GMO labeling is required and people can choose what they feed themselves and their families, they insisted that it was not possible to find enough non-GMO ingredients. They also felt that there was no consumer demand, even though we pointed out to them a *New York Times* poll[103] showing that 93 percent of people wanted GMO labeling along with numerous online petitions asking for Abbott to make non-GMO Similac.

After the dialogue had gotten nowhere, we had decided to escalate by filing a shareholder resolution, and it just so happened that Cari owned some shares of Abbott Laboratories. Within a few days, she had authorized us to file a shareholder resolution on her behalf.

"I knew I wanted to invest in responsible companies, but it never occurred to me that as a shareholder I had the power to transform corporate practices from the inside out," Rudd shared. She had more personal reasons for wanting to be involved in this particular cause, however.

"I had used Similac with my own son when he was an infant. In fact, it was given to us in a gift basket at the hospital," she said.

WILL MY FINANCIAL ADVISER TRY TO DISCOURAGE MY BEING AN ACTIVE SHAREHOLDER?

That was Cari Rudd's experience. "I contacted my financial adviser and told him what we planned to do," she said. "He did the equivalent of patting me on the head and saying, 'Now, don't you worry your pretty little head about that.'"

Unfortunately, this often occurs. Despite evidence to the contrary, some financial planners may believe that shareholder advocacy undermines the board of directors and may damage financial returns. Study after study has proven that this isn't true, but the financial establishment is slow to change.

Cari needed a document indicating that she and her husband had owned the Abbott stock for at least a year, and she isn't used to taking "no" for an answer. Since the adviser was less than helpful, she just asked his assistant for the document and got it without delay. This interaction showed her that maybe her financial advisor did not share some basic values. The bottom line is that you have a legal right to ask for and receive these documents in a timely way. If your advisor refuses or delays, you should formally complain to his/her supervisor.

CAN I SUBMIT A RESOLUTION MORE THAN ONCE?

Yes, and often it is necessary, as the Abbott initiative[104] demonstrates. In order to make the process more accessible to shareholders, the SEC has established minimum vote thresholds for proxy votes. The resolution submitted on Rudd's behalf[105] was simple and straightforward, essentially asking Abbott remove GMO ingredients from their products until they were proven safe or have an interim step to clearly label the ingredients.

Given the overwhelming level of support for labeling among consumers, we felt that shareholders would be responsive. But apparently Abbott shareholders aren't typical consumers. At their 2013 General Meeting, the resolution received just 3.2 percent of the vote. Although we were disappointed, the vote tally met the SEC threshold of 3 percent to permit the resolution to be resubmitted the following year.

Again, Rudd was the authorizing shareholder. This time, we upped the ante. In collaboration with SumofUs, an advocacy organization also working on this issue, a petition was circulated asking Abbott to market a non-GMO Similac product, or to label the one containing GMOs. The petition gathered some 70,000 signatures.

At the company's 2014 annual general meeting, we presented the petition. Circulating the petition gave both of our organizations an effective hook to seek news coverage of the issue, and as a result, the 2014 vote was better; the resolution earned a 6.2 percent favorable vote. This was enough to open the door a crack, but in subsequent discussions with Abbott, it was clear that they were not going to act. Still, the vote met SEC threshold of 6 percent to allow the resolution to be submitted again the following year.

This felt like *Groundhog Day*. Rudd authorized us to submit the resolution for a third time in 2015. We knew we needed 10 percent to continue—a high bar in this case. Without proxy advisors ISS or Glass Lewis supporting it, the resolution earned only a six percent favorable vote. The low approval rate meant that we'd have to wait three years before submitting it again.

That's a long time to wait, and, needless to say, our team and Rudd were disappointed. We examined the options available to us, but the situation didn't look good. Dialogue had failed. A petition had failed. The resolution had not gotten the results we'd hoped for on three occasions. It looked for the moment that Abbott would get a three-year reprieve.

But, as the saying goes, when a door closes, a window opens. This window was in the executive suite of Abbott Laboratories, and I wish we had the ability to look through it, because the company's next move came as a complete surprise to all of us.

In May 2015, Abbott announced that by the end of the month they would begin selling a "Similac Advance Non-GMO Infant Formula Powder" at Target. In a *New York Times*[106] article about the roll-out, Abbott cited consumer interest in the non-GMO products. Chris Calamari, general manager of Abbott's pediatric nutrition business, told the newspaper: "We listen to moms and dads, and they've told us they want a non-GMO option."

We were surprised and delighted by the move. The timing suggests that even as our third shareholder resolution was in play, the company was verifying the market research we had provided for them, possibly running focus groups, and finding suppliers for ingredients it would need to manufacture the product not just for a test market, as we had suggested, but nationwide at one of the country's largest retailers.

Figure 8: Polls show 93 percent of US consumers favor GMO labeling. After three shareholder resolutions Abbott Laboratories rolled out a non-GMO Similac for the US market. *Photo used with permission of the author.*

The Abbott decision-making process is opaque to us. However, I can't help but wonder whether, when Calamari told the *New York Times* that the company was responding to "moms and dads" who wanted a non-GMO option, he was referring to the moms and dads who participated in the polling and signed the petition we delivered at their annual general meeting.

The dialogue will continue so that shareholders can see how the market responds to the new product. We are confident that it will succeed, as within six months of the initial launch they added "Similac Advance Non-GMO Ready-to-Feed Liquid Formula," "Similac Sensitive Non-GMO Lactose Sensitive Powder," "Similac Go & Grow Non-GMO Toddler Drink Powder," and other variations. We hope that soon the company will add other nutritional products, including Ensure protein and nutrition drinks and bars for seniors, and dozens of protein products for hospital tube-fed patients.

IF YOU DO NOT GET THE MINIMUM RESOLUTION VOTE IS IT STILL WORTHWHILE?

Defining success in this arena has been long debated. Ultimately, the only measure that really matters is long-term change of corporate policies and practices.

As Abbott demonstrated, you don't need a high vote count to make change. Most votes are nonbinding, and true change happens at all vote levels. Shareholder resolutions are about bringing an idea to the public awareness, associating it with a brand, and encouraging corporate management to take action.

There are many examples of very high votes, majorities, and even near-unanimous votes that, on the one hand, were clear victories, but on the other did not affect short-term corporate policy shifts. In 2015 Royal Dutch Shell (RDS) and British Petroleum (BP) had 99 and 98 percent votes on greenhouse gas disclosure. In England, it should be noted, shareholder resolutions are binding and advocacy has a very different structure and tone. To file, a proponent needs either 100 shareholders or five percent of the outstanding shares, so resolutions are filed very infrequently. In this case a British group called "Aiming for A" built a coalition of 100+ shareholders and filed the resolutions. Management of both oil giants supported the resolutions, as they had been brought in early to have input on the drafting.

It would seem that the spirit of a 99 percent vote on climate change would have slowed Shell's pursuit of high-risk oil, but alas, a few weeks after the annual meeting the Royal Dutch Shell Polar Pioneer arctic drilling rig headed out of Seattle Harbor through hundreds of "kayaktivists"[107] engaged in the "paddle in Seattle."[108] The irony was that the rig returned shortly thereafter, and Shell's shareholders were hit with a $7 billion loss on the venture. Hopefully the disclosure that the two companies are required to provide will reshape their thinking and actions on climate change.

DOES WITHDRAWAL EQUAL VICTORY?

There are thousands of instances where engaging directly with a company has helped educate management and led to positive changes in corporate practices. Because of this many people believe that every withdrawal of a shareholder resolution equals victory. This is simply not the case. While true progress is often made in dialogue leading to a withdrawal, sometimes this is used as a stalling tactic by the company. Further, many proponents will not withdraw a proposal so that it goes to a vote for strategic reasons. The votes at annual meetings are reported in company filings to the SEC and become part of the public record, which means the company brand is forever associated with that specific ESG issue. Sometimes the fact that a company was warned by shareholders of an impending risk can be used years later in court during litigation, especially if the board ignores the warning of risk and a calamitous event occurs that was forewarned by astute shareholders.

Such an association is often the very thing that companies seek to avoid by negotiating for a withdrawal; advocates need to be willing to stay the course if the company is not willing to commit to specific, credible, and timely progress on the given issue.

Despite the fact that Cari's shareholder resolutions with Abbott didn't fully achieve what she desired, Rudd is eager to move forward on other initiatives. "The process was an empowering experience," she said. Her involvement had broader impact on her thinking about the power of shareholders, too. "In the back-and-forth of all this," she said, "I started to think about my mother, who doesn't have a college education and has worked very hard for an insurance company in Des Moines, Iowa, and has a 401(k). With the very modest life that she has, I kept thinking that she would feel so powerful if she could do something like this. It is an amazing avenue for just regular hardworking people."

Even though Rudd is an experienced investor with a long track record in political causes, she didn't really know what power she had before the shareholder resolution was filed. Discovering that power was, she said, "like you have a small garage, or a closet, and one day you find a big pry bar in there and you realize, 'Oh, my gosh, this can really do some work.'"

Rudd felt empowered by using her leverage as an investor. "I got my wish to 'own what I own,'" she said. "I got to understand the inner workings of how to press for change in a major global corporation as a shareholder and to witness the power shareholders and consumers have in advocating for practices that make a difference."

IF A WITHDRAWAL RESULTS IN A REPORT THAT IS INSUFFICIENT, WHAT DO YOU DO?

The 2013 As You Sow ExxonMobil filing[109] utilized shares owned by investor Martha Davis. Besides being an experienced investor, Davis was concerned about the long-term viability of her investments. However, she also had a more personal reason for getting involved in this particular action. She is a marine biologist who studies the conch, a marine gastropod native to the coasts of the Caribbean, the Florida Keys, the Bahamas, and Bermuda. She regularly travels to those areas where she and other divers conduct a census of the animals, recording their numbers, size, range, and the conditions of their habitat. In recent years, she has noticed an alarming decline in the conch population, which she attributes to overfishing and changes in the marine environment that may be linked to carbon dioxide in the atmosphere caused by the burning of fossil fuels. The ocean absorbs carbon dioxide, and as CO_2 levels rise, so does the acidity of seawater, which in turn causes coral and mollusk shells to weaken.

When As You Sow's President and Chief Counsel Danielle Fugere and Arjuna Capital's Director of Equity Research and Shareholder Engagement Natasha Lamb sat down with the ExxonMobil negotiators, the company requested that the resolution be withdrawn.

Fugere and Lamb refused, confident that the resolution would receive a significant favorable vote if it went on the proxy ballot. ExxonMobil clearly didn't want to take that risk if they didn't have to. Negotiations, often very contentious, continued until finally an agreement was reached: the resolution would be withdrawn in exchange for ExxonMobil's commitment to issue a report on Carbon Asset Risk, addressing the eleven areas of concern[110] focused on exactly what the risk to shareholders was from stranded assets and how ExxonMobil intended to thrive in a carbon-constrained future.

Of course, the company could—and should—do more. But ExxonMobil's agreement was an important first step, and it was achieved without the shareholder resolution coming to a vote. That remains in her arsenal—and ExxonMobil knows that.

Perhaps a strong vote favoring the shareholder resolution would have been more satisfying, but ExxonMobil's agreement was significant in that it represented the first time that a major fossil fuel company had agreed to be forthcoming with their worldview about how climate change might restrict them from developing all their fossil fuel assets.

When the "Energy and Carbon—Managing the Risks"[111] report was published, stating, "We are confident that none of our hydrocarbon reserves are now or will become 'stranded,'" we sent out a press release commending the company for releasing a report, but pointed out that the data was insufficient.

The report made the *New York Times*[112] front-page business section. The lack of disclosure sent a ripple through Wall Street and was picked up by over 400 other press outlets. So sometimes the disclosure, or lack thereof, even if not what you asked for, has profound repercussions.

FIRST THERE IS A MOUNTAIN

One ringside witness to those changes is Sanford Lewis, an attorney with over 30 years of experience in public policy–related issues, including environmental law, securities law, and public policy campaigns. He's also a leading national expert on the filing and defense of shareholder resolutions and has been an eyewitness to their evolution.

A couple of years ago, he was involved when the New York State Common Retirement Fund filed a resolution asking a company involved in coal extraction using mountaintop removal to submit disclosures about the environmental impact of their activities.

In response, the company filed what Lewis characterized as "a detailed legalistic challenge" to the proposal, asserting, in essence, that they were not engaged in the practice of mountaintop removal at all, so the proposal was not relevant to them. In support, the company submitted what Lewis characterized as a "twisted" legal definition of mountaintop removal drawn from coal mining regulations.

Lewis's response was a document illustrated with ten pages of before-and-after photos. One picture would show a mountain. Another picture would show the same location. No mountain. At that point, Lewis said, "The SEC could not agree with them that they were not doing mountaintop removal." In this case, Lewis successfully challenged the claim that the proposal was not relevant to the company.

Figure 9: The US Environmental Protection Agency studied more than 1,200 stream segments impacted by mountaintop mining and reported zinc, sodium, selenium, and sulfate levels in local streams. *Photo used with permission of Dave Cooper, The Mountaintop Removal Roadshow.*

CHAPTER

10

The Power of Disclosure

What do you need as a shareholder to make informed investment decisions? In short, you need material information, and thanks to shareholder advocates, there is more information available than ever before.

EXECUTIVE COMPENSATION
SPIRALING OUT OF CONTROL

One prime example pertains to executive compensation. According to the AFL-CIO's 2014 Executive Pay Watch report, the average CEO earns $11.7 million ($5,625/hour), or 331 times the average worker's salary. Compared to a minimum wage worker ($7.75/hour), the average CEO earns a staggering 775 times more. To put that into context, it would take the minimum wage worker nearly *eight centuries* to earn as much as does the average CEO in one year. This isn't a problem that started yesterday. Over the past 35 years, CEO pay has grown some 937 percent.[113] Meanwhile, worker salaries have remained almost flat since the 1970s, increasing a meager inflation-adjusted 2.6 percent for the 12-month period ending March 2015, according the Bureau of Labor Statistics.

As You Sow is fighting excessive CEO compensation with disclosure, by annually publishing *The 100 Most Overpaid CEOs*[114] report that details the scale of CEO pay and—of importance to shareholders—the disconnect with performance.

The report establishes that many chief executives are getting raises while the companies they lead are failing. Some manipulate stock price with buybacks to inflate their stock options. We believe that direct and detailed disclosure of this kind of information can have a powerful effect to influence shareholders as they work to hold boards accountable.

Disproportionate compensation is not good for the companies, the shareholders, the customers, the other employees, the economy, or society as a whole.

You Deserve a Raise Today: Feeling the pressure of income disparity, some companies are making an effort to correct the imbalance. In February 2015 McDonald's announced that it would increase the wages of some 90,000 employees in company-owned stores by $1 per hour over the local minimum wage.[116] That same month, Walmart—the world's largest retailer—announced that some 500,000 of its full-time and part-time employees would receive pay raises to at least $9 an hour—$1.75 above the federal minimum wage. That's a step in the right direction. These are hopeful signs, but by no means do these examples solve the broader problem. Pay rates are still way out of balance, and many Walmart employees are living below or just at the poverty line, receiving food-stamps that they spend at Walmart[117]—essentially a subsidy for the world's largest retailer, courtesy of the American taxpayers.

SAY ON PAY

After many years of shareholder resolutions requesting that companies disclose CEO pay and allow shareholders to vote on it, the 2010 Dodd-Frank Act put it into law. The "Say on Pay" rule allows shareholders to vote on executive compensation. Shareholders decide if they vote every one, two, or three years.

The assumption is that putting CEO pay packages on the proxy ballot and having full disclosure about those packages would help bring CEOs under control. Many proponents thought that CEOs would be shamed by the public disclosure of their outsized compensation. Unfortunately, greed took hold instead, with executives demanding that they be paid more than their peers. CEO pay rates have spiraled out of control even more rapidly since the enactment of the rule.

As is often the case, ordinary people are well ahead of institutions in understanding the problem. The anti-poverty charity Oxfam warned leaders in Davos at the World Economic Forum that that the combined wealth of the richest one percent will overtake that of the other 99 percent of people in 2016 unless the current trend of rising inequality is checked.[115]

MORE DISCLOSURE NEEDED ON POLITICAL SPENDING

Executive compensation is only one component of the disclosures that shareholders have a right to demand. Full disclosure of political spending, which is currently unlimited thanks to the Supreme Court decision known as *Citizens United*, is also needed.[118] The court ruling said political spending is protected under the First Amendment, meaning corporations and unions could spend unlimited amounts of money on political activities, aslong as it was done independently of a party or candidate. Much of that money remains hidden from shareholders as it is channeled through trade organizations and political action committees.

The leading shareholder advocacy organization focused on this issue is the Center for Political Accountability.[119] Their president and founder Bruce Freed created, in collaboration with the Zicklin Center for Business Ethics Research at University of Pennsylvania Wharton School, the CPA-Zicklin Index that "benchmarks the political disclosure and accountability policies and practices of leading US public companies." It is issued annually with updated scores for public companies as they move up the scale toward true transparency.

DIVERSITY EQUALS BETTER RETURNS

Executive compensation and political spending are only two issues that shareholders can address. Another one—board diversity—is also critical to keeping American corporations competitive, nimble, and responsive to the changing global business environment.

It was an understatement when the *New York Times* recently called US public company boards, "pale, male, and stale."[120] According to a recent *Forbes* article,[121] the boards of the Fortune 100 companies are 92 percent male, with a median age of 57. Women hold just 16.6 percent of board seats at Fortune 500 companies, and many companies have none.

In contrast to the United States, the European Union mandates that boards be composed of 30 percent women, with Norway and Finland requiring 40 percent.[122]

But is board diversity good for business? A 2012 Credit Suisse study[123] says it is. Among the findings published in *Gender Diversity and Corporate Performance*, the banking giant said that "in testing the performance of 2,360 companies globally over the last six years, our analysis shows that it would on average have been better with women on their management boards than in those without."

It's unlikely that corporate boards will voluntarily diversify, and government quotas and other "top-down" dictates are even less probable, so shareholders will have to pressure corporate boards to take action, and they can make a very compelling business case according to the *Forbes* article, "Top 10 Reasons

Diversity Is Good For The Boardroom"[124]: "board diversity is simply smart business . . . it's nothing short of irresponsible for chief executives not to place their board composition under the microscope."

Among the reasons why companies with diverse boards outperform is that their board reflects the real world and represents different perspectives and potential markets that can lead to a healthy internal debate and possibly reduce risk and increase opportunity. In addition, people from divergent backgrounds tackle the same problems in different ways, coming to better solutions. According to *Forbes*, it will lead to improved reputation and brand associations and make the company more adaptable to its ever-changing environment.

Recognizing both the social and financial benefits of increasing board diversity and working with the Thirty Percent Coalition,[125] in 2012 Trillium Asset Management began engaging portfolio companies with all-male boards and those lagging its peers on diversity. Over three years Trillium engaged 16 companies through shareholder proposals and dialogues asking companies to "publicly commit [themselves] to a policy of board inclusiveness to ensure that women are routinely sought as part of every board search the company undertakes."[126]

Following successful dialogues, resolutions were withdrawn at eight companies including Chipotle Mexican Grill, Citrix, eBay, PaloAlto Networks, and AngioDynamics that agreed to amend their governance documents to include a clear definition of diversity, inclusive of gender and race, and to make diversity an intentional part of board nominee search criteria. Seven other companies including Apple, Lowe's, and eBay, as well as lesser-known firms like Zimmer, Cree, and Superior Energy agreed to make the legal commitments, and actually added women to their boards. One of the most remarkable changes came at Hartford Financial, where over the course of two years the company added three women onto its board, making a total of four out of 11 and representing 36 percent.

WHAT CAN BE DONE WITH INFORMATION ONCE IT IS DISCLOSED?

As an aid to investors and an incentive to industries to improve their practices, shareholder advocates have sought disclosure and generated reports on issues including carbon footprint,[127] beverage container recycling,[128] toxic chemicals in foods,[129] Bisphenol A (BPA) in the lining of cans,[130] and hydraulic fracturing.[131] Advocates have also demanded that corporations produce their own sustainability reports. Corporate sustainability reporting is now a standard practice, with 75 percent of the S&P 500 index publishing reports.[132]

As Bob Massie, Ceres Executive Director from 1996 to 2002, put it, "The whole idea of having an environmental ethic, or measuring your performance above and beyond your legal requirements, was considered completely insane. Sustainability was considered to be a shockingly difficult thing that no company would ever voluntarily take on as a goal."[133]

Disclosure is foundational, but it is not an end in itself. It allows for the establishment of baselines, comparative practices, and determination of rankings. The ultimate goal is to influence corporate policy that translates into operational change, first at companies that lag behind, and then across an industry. Active shareholders can participate in many phases of this process.

DOES NEGATIVE PUBLICITY SPUR COMPANIES AHEAD?

Creating a scorecard to compare companies is a prime example of how to separate leaders from laggards to move an industry. Motivated by poor US bottle/can recycling rates, As You Sow first published a report ranking corporate commitments to beverage container recycling in 2006. In that report, Nestlé Waters NA, the largest US water company, was cited as a laggard, and earned a dismal F.

CEO Kim Jeffery started making changes soon after the scorecard was released, and in 2008, with the release of the second scorecard, Nestlé Waters moved up to a C–. In 2009, they committed to a goal of recycling 60 percent of their polyethylene terephthalate (PET) beverage containers by 2018.

The company also conveyed to As You Sow that the report card had opened their eyes to their lack of sustainability practices.

"Over the past two years, As You Sow engaged Nestlé Waters North America in a respectful but insistent dialogue on container recycling," said Alex McIntosh, director of corporate citizenship for Nestlé Waters. "Its 2006 container recycling report and scorecard got our attention and encouraged us to look at the recycling challenge more broadly. As a result, our company has developed

Figure 10: 2006 Beverage Report Scorecard. *Used with permission of As You Sow.*

a deeper understanding of the challenges and opportunities of improving container recycling rates and recycled content, and has helped us adopt a bolder vision and commitment to comprehensive recycling in the US."

In 2010, PepsiCo, not to be outdone by Coke or Nestle Waters, committed to recycle 50 percent of all industry bottles and cans by 2018.

The third report, in 2011, had Coke, Pepsi, and Nestlé Waters in a three-way tie for first place, each earning a B–. The fourth report in 2015 expanded to include fast food and consumer packaging. All three beverage companies, plus New Belgium Brewing, were ranked in the "Better Practices" category, with programs that mean 40 to 50 billion fewer plastic bottles will end up landfilled or polluting the oceans of world.

But there is still room for improvement. None of the companies made "Best Practices," and the goal of recycling 100 percent of the 250 billion plastic bottles produced each year in North America is still some distance off. The goal is to establish "extended producer responsibility[134] (EPR)," or similar product stewardship policies where companies agree to take financial responsibility for part or all of the costs to collect and recycle their products or packaging. It is the law of the land in a number of European countries[135] and results in recycling rates as high as 80 percent.

HOW DO YOU MAKE SURE THEY DO WHAT THEY PROMISED?

Since most shareholder resolutions are nonbinding, backsliding is a recurring risk. Competition, market conditions, or management may change, or maybe the short-term costs of keeping their promises have too great an impact on their quarterly reports.

That's why steady and persistent follow-up is required. Shareholder advocates have had significant success using scorecards and reports to keep pressure on companies by documenting when they have kept their promises and when they have not.

Press coverage can be a tremendous aid in keeping corporations' feet to the fire, but the first step may not be to accuse them of lying in the press. Instead, letting a corporation know that you're about to launch a press release detailing how the company has failed to keep its word may be a way to provide powerful incentive to a corporation to clean up its act. Pointing out competitors' compliance with a given practice can also provide a powerful motivation to reform.

Levels of escalation from there might be to request further negotiation so they can correct the problem, with the underlying understanding that you retain the option to file another shareholder resolution, knowing that you can build shareholder engagement by pointing out the company's failure to follow through on their promises.

11

Divestment as the Ultimate Escalation of Engagement

You want to make change. You engaged with the company by writing and meeting with them. You filed a shareholder resolution and took it to the annual general meeting. You voted your proxy, and your resolution got a decent vote. But the company—in fact, the whole industry—is simply continuing with business as usual. What else can you do?

Paul Neuhauser's shareholder resolutions with General Motors, asking the company to cease business in South Africa, shows that time and again, shareholders working together can bring about meaningful and lasting reforms. In the case of South Africa, a critical component that led to the fall of apartheid was a worldwide divestment campaign against firms doing business in South Africa. In this case, divestment was the tactic that ignited a movement that led to change.

There is a long history of shareholders using divestment as a powerful tool, from divestment of companies doing business with the apartheid regime in South Africa to divestment of companies engaged in pornography, tobacco, and the Sudan. It is a statement that you refuse to profit from the activities that a particular company or group of companies participate in. It is the ultimate shareholder escalation. It says that the company does not have the moral right to exist.

As we have seen, being a shareholder gives you a seat at the table. Engaged shareholders have brought about positive reforms in the environmental, social, and governance of hundreds of corporations. However, in many cases, and today in the case of fossil fuel companies that continue business as usual while denying that they are complicit in the global peril of climate change, divestment has become a powerful global mobilizing force.

In 2010 Wallace Global Fund's Executive Director Ellen Dorsey and Program Director Richard Mott commissioned As You Sow to write a divest fossil fuel strategy paper to link the fiduciary duty of university endowments, foundations, and pension funds with the reality that coal, oil, and gas companies were creating moral and financial risk to these institutions. The divestment strategy white paper was distributed to a small group of nongovernmental organizations (NGOs) that were brought together to develop a divest fossil fuel action plan, create a campus toolkit, and train and place organizers on college campuses to help students demand that their university endowments divest from coal. These groups included Responsible Endowments Coalition, Environmental Integrity Project, Earth Justice, Sierra Club Student Coalition, Energy Action Coalition, Sustainable Endowments Institute, Southern Alliance for Clean Energy, and As You Sow.

The first campuses targeted were the University of North Carolina at Chapel Hill and the University of Illinois at Urbana-Champaign. The movement caught fire on its own at Swarthmore, and more organizers were dispatched to Brown, Lewis & Clark, Duke, NYU, Yale, and other universities. The call to action was simple—the mission of a university is to create a safe and prosperous future for their students, but by investing in fossil fuels, they were profiting from the very companies that were dooming their students to a decimated planet, a collapsed economy, and global chaos.

The Carbon Tracker stranded assets concept added economic data to the argument, and when 350.org's Bill McKibben published his "Global Warming's Terrifying New Math"[136] article in *Rolling Stone* in July 2012, and went on a 21-city "Do the Math" road show,[137] the campus movement exploded to over 300 campuses in a few months. The civil action grew rapidly and was soon supported by organizations from across a broad spectrum, linking climate change to justice, faith, and health. These leaders who joined the divest-invest movement included Rev. Lennox Yearwood Jr., President and CEO of the Hip Hop Caucus,[138] Rev. Fletcher Harper, Executive Director of Green Faith,[139] and Gary Cohen President and Co-Founder of Health Care Without Harm.[140]

Meanwhile, Wallace Global organized a core group of foundations to create, "Divest Invest Philanthropy"[141] and sign the divest-invest pledge that committed them to move capital away from industries destroying the planet and into those building a clean energy future.

In 2013, 17 foundations, including Wallace Global Foundation, Schmidt Family Foundation, Park Foundation, Russell Family Foundation, Merck Family Foundation, Compton Foundation, and the Educational Foundation of America, totaling almost two billion dollars in assets, launched Divest-Invest Philanthropy.[142]

By September 2014 the UN climate march hit the streets of New York City, with over 400,000 people representing all sectors of civil society from around the world. At that gathering the divest-invest pledge total had grown to $50 billion.[143] It made headlines when the Rockefeller Brothers Fund, a foundation founded with Standard Oil and Exxon money, signed the divest-invest pledge[144] committing to sell all investments in fossil fuels, including their holdings of ExxonMobil. In addition, giving a push to foundations, actor Mark Ruffalo added his celebrity power and David Blood added the investment prowess of Generation Investment Management to elevate a movement in its infancy. Soon, Stanford University[145] and the Norwegian government pension fund,[146] the world's largest sovereign wealth fund, with assets of $900 billion, both committed to divest from coal and tar sands. A year later in September 2015, the assets under management hit $2.6 trillion, with celebrities like Leonardo

DiCaprio joining the group.[147] The total assets under management of organizations and individuals that had signed the divest-invest pledge jumped to $3.4 trillion[148] by December at the UN Paris climate summit.

Divestment is a statement, an affirmation that the companies causing the problem cannot continue to recklessly destroy our future while they block policy and progress to solve the problem. It says that business as usual is not acceptable.

There is another aspect to the divestment movement: the financial risk aspect. This is what stranded assets are all about—risk. During this period of time the coal industry lost over 80 percent of its value, as dramatically shown in the value of a coal ETF with the ticker KOL dropping from $50.00/share to $7.00/share.[149] This fall is attributable to a number of factors, including the plummeting costs of natural gas, the advent of price-competitive renewable energy, and the necessary environmental controls on the burning of coal, making the retirement of old plants needing expensive scrubber technology a certainty. Thousands of investors lost billions of dollars in capital in the collapse of the coal industry, and there is no real reason to expect a turnaround. For that reason the complete divestment from coal is the only reasonable course.

To look at the collapse of coal stocks is to glimpse the future of oil and gas. Since August 2014, a glut of oil on the market has pushed down oil prices from $112 per barrel to under $35 per barrel in December 2015—an eleven-year low.

However, the price of oil is not the only reason that fossil fuel company stocks are underperforming. In fact, they have been faltering for the past five years, and without stock buybacks to keep stock prices inflated, without huge debt to pay dividends,[150, 151] and with costs of searching for ever more expensive reserves increasing more rapidly than revenue, the house of cards is set to collapse, and the myth that fossil fuel demand will increase endlessly into the future will be overturned.

Some very prominent investors and institutions have divested without making a public statement. This action, known as "closet divesting," reduces their financial carbon risk but does not make the powerful statement associated with divestment. A few examples of this include Warren Buffett, who sold all of his shares from two oil and gas majors—ExxonMobil Corp. and ConocoPhillips—worth $3.87 billion and $36 million, respectively in the fourth quarter of 2014. The Bill and Melinda Gates Foundation sold its entire ExxonMobil position, too, jettisoning $765.9 million in stock. George Soros got out of ExxonMobil, as well, shedding $88 million worth of the stock through a put option.[152]

The most held mutual fund in all US 401(k) plans, Vanguard Institutional Index Fund Institutional Shares (VINIX), quietly divested from coal as did many other major funds. In addition, Securities and Exchange Commission filings detail how the Harvard Management Company Inc., which oversees a small slice of the university's finances, sold all its shares of Kinder Morgan Energy Partners LP, an oil services and transportation firm, amounting to a $97 million sale. Yet Harvard still publicly fights their own students on this issue.

Meanwhile, the University of Dayton, led by trustee George Hanley, became the first Catholic institution to divest, foreshadowing what the Vatican would do a few months later. In the spring of 2015 the pope issued his Encyclical "Laudato si,"[153] making a moral call to do everything possible to avert climate change and protect the Earth.

In April of 2016, according to the *Yale Daily News*, Chief Investment Officer David Swensen added climate change awareness to Yale's investment strategy. Swensen reported that after months of talking with Yale's external investment managers about the potential risks associated with investments in coal and oil, around $10 million of the endowment has been removed from two publicly-traded fossil fuel producers. He said that by the end of Fiscal Year 2015, Yale's $25.6 billion endowment had only minor exposure to the oil and coal industries.[154]

Adding to the divestment movement, Citibank pledged to invest and facilitate a total of $100 billion within the next 10 years to finance activities that reduce the impacts of climate change.[155] JP Morgan Chase claims to have cut coal investments by 50 percent and multiplied cleantech investments six-fold.

Do these major investors and banking institutions know something that corporate risk committees don't? Yes! Namely, that climate change has the potential to disrupt or destroy their business.

However, if you're not Bill Gates, Warren Buffett, or a trustee of the Rockefeller Brothers Foundation, how do you draw attention to your divestment strategy? First of all, sign the pledge at Divest-Invest Individual.[156] If you want to keep engaging and voting your proxy, the divest-invest pledge specifically allows for the holding of enough stock to continue engagement with the company. At the Paris climate talks, where the pledge number jumped to over $3.4 trillion, there was general consensus that it was time to exit fossil fuel investments for both financial and moral reasons and to use this moral authority to pressure these companies to transition their business plans or wind down operations.

12

How Do I Know
What I Own?

Most people know the companies that they hold as direct equities. But very few know which company stocks
are embedded in their retirement plans, 401(k), 403(b), mutual
funds, ETFs, and other investing vehicles. This is why we built a
free, open-to-the-public web tool specifically designed to compare fund holdings with any given list based on ESG criteria.
The first version is called Fossil Free Funds.[157] A gender diversity, gun, and prison version will be developed soon. These tools
are described in detail in the next chapter.

The fundamental takeaway is that those who divest and those
who engage have the same goal, and divestment and engagement
strategies strengthen each other by using market forces to bring
about change. As Executive Secretary of the UN Framework
Convention on Climate Change,[158] Christiana Figueres said in
a recent *New Yorker* article, "Where capital goes over the next
fifteen years is going to decide whether we're actually able to
address climate change and what kind of a century we are going
to have.[159]

The first step is to find out what those investments are—and
it isn't quite as simple as just asking. In the global economy, many
investment vehicles seem to have opted for maximum complexity

and opacity, so it's often difficult to determine, first of all, what companies are held within various indexes, mutual funds, and ETFs. Once you know, it's also very difficult to tell if these companies—regardless of their public statements—are actually aligned with your values.

We built a web tool to enable transparency on any environmental, social, or governance issue and, as of the writing of this book, have deployed one related to climate change. We also have one for gender—specifically the number of women on the boards of the companies within any given fund.

The way it works is that you type your fund name or ticker into the search bar shown above, and instantly you see the number and names of companies that have zero, 30 percent, or 50 percent female board members. Below is what you would see if you set the threshold at 30 for companies in an ETF called SPY from State Street that tracks the S&P 500. Note that 444 out of 500, or 86 percent, do not make the cut, including Apple, Microsoft, and Exxon.

Figure 11: Gender diversity on corporate boards can be screened in your mutual funds. *Used with permission of As You Sow and iStock Photo.*

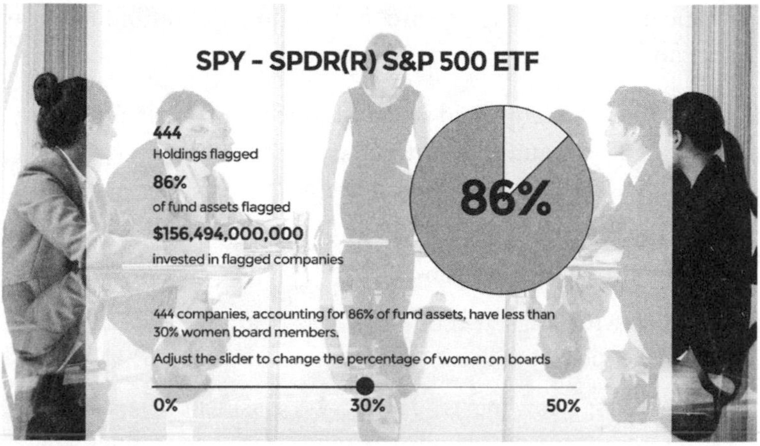

Figure 12: 86 percent or 444 of the Fortune 500 companies have less than 30 percent women board members. *Used with permission of As You Sow and iStock Photo*

We also built a version to enable anyone to see the fossil fuel companies in their fund holdings. With human-caused climate change being a profound and acknowledged threat, investors with assets worth over $3.4 trillion[160] have signed a pledge[161] to divest from fossil fuel stocks and invest in a clean energy future. The majority of those assets are held by pensions, sovereign wealth funds, endowments, and foundations. Additionally, over 50,000 individuals have also signed the pledge.[162] It is growing every day.[163] The vast majority of these people have pledged to divest from fossil fuel companies but cannot act on that pledge, as they have no idea how climate complicit they are because they do not know what they own.

HOW THE PLATFORM WORKS

Fossil Free Funds offers analysis of the 3,000 mutual funds that are held in the most US 401(k) plans. As the common definition of *fossil free* is evolving, the platform will allow anyone to screen against five accepted lists and standardized industry classifications, building toward a common definition. You can select and deselect for any combination of:

- Carbon Underground 200™: Largest 100 coal and largest 100 oil and gas companies as measured by proven reserves factored for carbon intensity
- Filthy 15: Ten largest coal-fired utilities and five largest coal extraction companies
- Coal: Morningstar Industry Classification—coal mining companies
- Oil/Gas: Morningstar Industry Classification—oil and gas companies, including exploration and refinement, service industry, pipelines, and smaller extraction companies
- Fossil-Fired Utilities: Morningstar Standardized Business Classification of utilities with 100 percent renewable power generators removed

A BRIEF TOUR

The Fossil Free Funds financial transparency web tool allows users to search through a database of mutual funds to see what portion of the fund is comprised of fossil fuel companies. The interface is very simple: two levels enable users to enter any one of 3,000 mutual funds into the search bar. In the screengrab below, the fund that is held in the most 401(k) plans, Vanguard Value Index I, with the ticker "VINIX," was searched.

This takes you to a second level that instantly shows the Carbon Underground 200 (CU200) companies in the selected fund. In the case below, note that 4.65 percent of this fund's holdings are in the CU200. If you go to the website and run this search, you will see much more detail than we can show in the screenshot below. There are 24 companies sorted by weighting: ExxonMobil at 1.89 percent, Chevron at .95 percent, and so on. You can unfurl the list to see all 24.

Figure 13: Type in a ticker or fund name and discover the fossil fuel companies embedded in your mutual funds and 401(k) plan. *Used with permission of As You Sow and Indigo Creative Design. Background photos used with permission of Fuse, Corbis, Getty Images and Olga Khoroshunova, Hemera, and Thinkstock.*

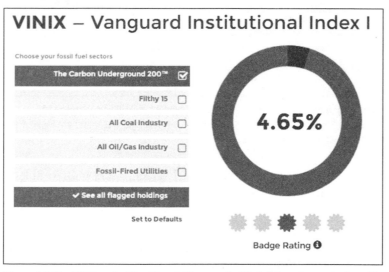

Figure 14: The VINIX mutual fund has 4.65 percent of its holdings in companies with the largest reserves of coal, oil, and gas. *Used with permission of As You Sow.*

By selecting the four other options below the text, "Choose Your Fossil Fuel Sectors," users self-define "fossil free." They can select any combination or all of them if they want to see all the coal, oil, gas, service industries, and utilities.

As the screen below shows, if all fossil fuel sectors are selected, VINIX has 11.32 percent fossil fuel companies. On the actual website you will see that this is 72 companies total, worth $21 billion. The largest holding is ExxonMobil at 1.89 percent; next is Berkshire at 1.34 percent, and so on.

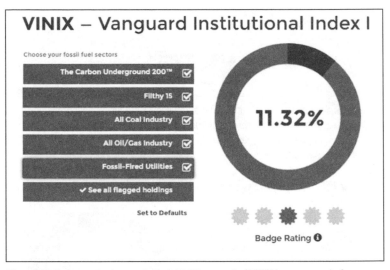

Figure 15: A deeper look reveals that 11.32 percent of VINIX is composed of companies that have fossil reserves, provide extraction services, and are fossil-fired utilities. *Used with permission of As You Sow.*

By customizing their fossil fuel screen, users will be able to easily see which companies in a mutual fund are contrary to their personal values.

By sourcing mutual fund data from Morningstar and screening against lists like Fossil Free Indexes' Carbon Underground 200, the Fossil Free Funds tool shines a light on the murky world of investment vehicles. This free website enables individual and institutional investors to have instant access to the information necessary to divest from fossil fuels and construct a portfolio that aligns with specific divestment and investment objectives. We believe that what is transparent can be transformed.

13

How to Get Your Company to Offer Funds Aligned with Your Values

This chapter is based on the input and review of three experts in this area: R. Paul Herman, founder and CEO of HIP Investor,[164] Rob Thomas of Social(k),[165] and Timothy Yee of Green Retirement.[166]

You've used one of the transparency tools available to understand what you own, looked inside your employer-sponsored retirement plan mutual fund holdings, and have determined that you want to make some changes. So what's next?

If your investments are in your employer-sponsored plan at work, it is possible to change what the plan offers, but it will take more effort than if you have a personal investment you control. You will need to engage the plan administrator to help find the right blend of funds to satisfy the many employees that all invest in the same basket of mutual funds. This may take time and possibly some coordination with your co-plan participants.

STEP 1: TALK TO YOUR COLLEAGUES

To effectively advocate for new offerings through your employer-sponsored plan, first build a coalition of peers and interested co-workers inside your company. Your voice will be much stronger as a group. If you're writing to someone in power, advocating on behalf of 10 or even 20 people carries a lot more weight than just one. One way to spur interest would be sharing the results from your search among fellow employees. All plan participants are offered the same basket of funds as you are, so they are probably asking the same questions right now. It will certainly make interesting conversation around the water cooler.

Some companies have social justice, human rights, or green teams, and there may be affinity groups for gender equality or LGBT employees, and if there isn't one already, it may be time to create one for a specific issue, be it human rights or environmental health. Communicate with your co-workers through a company intranet, employee portal, a company newsletter, corporate chats, or social media. The herd is heard!

STEP 2: IDENTIFY THE BEST PEOPLE IN THE COMPANY TO SPEAK WITH

The 401(k)/403(b)[167] plan administrator, manager, or coordinator should be known if you are a plan participant, and that's where to start. There could also be a chief sustainability officer or employee engagement manager, and those could be good resources. An effective method is to go to the LinkedIn pages of those people and find who might have some sympathy for the cause. Do any of them volunteer or have connections with organizations concerned with climate change? Look for indicators that they're friendly to sustainability and start contacting them in order of their friendliness. In a publicly listed company with more structure, a coalition is vital to signal to managers that it's an important issue for many employees. If it's a smaller company, the CFO or CEO could be approached directly. In a midsize or family company, a family member could be more influential.

STEP 3: BRING A SOLUTION TO THE TABLE

The usual starting point in these conversations is, "We want to reduce the future risk of our 401(k) fund choices. We also want to invest in funds aligned with our values, like funds that support gender diversity and don't have fossil fuels. How can we enhance our 401(k) choices to do so?" Here are the criteria. Getting three new fund choices added to the list of the existing 15 to 30 is a formal process and could take a year to be added. Larger companies often have some form of investment committee that engages an investment advisor. There may be some funds in your plan that you see contain only one company you feel is out of alignment. You could ask the plan administrator to call the fund manager and say, "Is there a substitute for this one company?"

If the investment advisor and plan administrator refuse to help in swapping out some funds for others, you may need to get fellow employees to sign a petition requesting the change and send it to the investment committee. If you are told, "But you'll make less money," you can reply, "Actually companies with women on the boards outperform those without, according to a Credit Suisse report,[168] and oil is very risky these days. We want to diversify, and reduce our risk."

IF YOU ARE AN INDIVIDUAL INVESTOR

If you are not part of a workplace plan, it is much easier to divest and reinvest; it's your money, and you can trade on your own using E*TRADE or a similar platform, or there is a financial advisor who works for you. You just need to have a meeting to discuss what you have learned about your holdings and how you would like them changed to align with your values. An investment professional will advise you of potential risk, and you can make your own decisions. If you ask your advisor to make changes and you get push-back telling you that you'll make lower returns, then dive deeper into the discussion, as this may be a knee-jerk reaction and not based on current data.

Your advisor may recommend against investing in a specific fund because it has a short or rocky history, so you may need to be patient while your advisor finds a better alternative. The goal is to reduce risk and align with your values, and there are many ways to do this. If the advisor is unwilling to help you with this transition, it may be time to find a new advisor.

Not everyone has time to vet their investments, let alone file shareholder resolutions or take other actions. However, if you're concerned that your investment dollars are not working toward goals that you support, you can choose a Socially Responsible Investment advisor, also known as "Sustainable, Responsible, Impact Investing," "socially conscious," "mission," "green," or "ethical" wealth manager to guide you. The overarching term is an advisor who considers environmental, social, and governance (ESG) issues.

These investment advisors seek out investments that comply with set criteria: for example, they might seek investments that are involved with human rights, LGBT rights, sustainable forests, consumer protection, or labor rights, to name a few. You can find out much more about these firms at US SIF or the Forum for Sustainable and Responsible Investing.[169]

Individual companies are "screened" or removed from your portfolio in one of three ways. Negative screens filter out companies that are involved in a certain sector or sectors of the economy: the use of animal testing in their products, for example.

Positive screens add investments according to desired criteria: companies that have more than 30 percent women on the boards, do not do testing on animals, and have signed a pledge to not buy cotton harvested with child slave labor, for example.

A restricted screen allows a certain small percentage of undesirable activity within a company. These are also referred to as "best of class." Investors may support the companies that are leaders in their sector and move investments away from laggards. We are seeing a great deal of this in the utility sector as companies shift their energy mix to renewables but still may burn some gas and coal. These are often chosen over those continuing to burn coal. Companies that get a good grade in a report on recycling or make public statements about offering a fair living wage are often rewarded with investments.

As a component of SRI investment, dozens of Mutual Funds and ETFs—Exchange Traded Funds—have also been created so that one can invest in hundreds of equities that meet designated environmental, social, and governance criteria. But just because an investment meets ESG criteria does not guarantee returns. There are good ESG investors and bad ones, just like there are good and bad investment advisors and fund managers in the world of non-SRI investing.

Also, the advisor should either be actively involved in proxy voting and filing or co-filing ESG-issue shareholder proposals or at least be supportive of the concept and its potential to reform corporate practices. Shareholder advocacy, plus impact investing and fully integrating ESG factors across your entire portfolio, are the three pillars to build a holistic and empowered approach to investment that reflects an alignment between your values and your portfolio.

14

A New Generation of Corporate Leaders

I don't know if corporate boards can ever plan seven generations ahead, but having been granted the advantages of personhood, corporations should at least be directed by their shareholders to conduct themselves as responsible "people" of a larger community. Shareholder advocates can push them to do it, but some CEOs are accepting that challenge of their own accord.

NEAR-DEATH WAKE-UP CALL

Several years ago, recovering from a near-death experience, Aetna Insurance CEO Mark Bertolini began meditating and doing yoga.[170] He found the practices so beneficial that he rolled out meditation and yoga classes in the company's offices. Some 13,000 employees—a quarter of the work force—have now taken part.

Class participants reported reduced stress, a 20 percent improvement in sleep quality, and a reduction in pain of 19 percent. In terms of investment return, class participants gained an average of 62 minutes per week of productivity, which the company, Aetna, estimated was worth $3,000 annually per employee. Medical visits and prescription drug use were also down by some 30 percent, resulting in enormous savings.

That's the kind of bottom line payoff that CEOs love and that boards should recognize and reward. Aetna's program has been so successful that it has begun selling the classes to clients and offering reduced premiums for participants.

Bertolini isn't alone in this sort of consciousness-raising management. There are emotional intelligence courses at Google. At General Mills' corporate campus, every building has a meditation room. Employees at the Wall Street firms BlackRock and Goldman Sachs can take advantage of free meditation classes.

Bertolini didn't stop with meditation, however. After reading *Capital in the Twenty-First Century*, a book about wealth and income inequality by French economist Thomas Piketty, he also took the wage disparity issue by the horns, increasing pay by 33 percent to $16 per hour for Aetna's lowest-paid employees. Bertolini is on the record as saying that even if the raise didn't make strict economic sense, he was still glad he put it in place, because it was the right thing to do for his company's employees.

"Doing the right thing" was behind the move by CVS Health, operators of the CVS drugstore chain, to halt sales of tobacco products in 2014. In keeping with its mission to promote better health, the company launched stop-smoking programs. Several months later, CVS, with 7,800 stores nationwide, quit the US Chamber of Commerce in protest of the Chamber's strong-arm tactics in promoting smoking outside the country. Shifts like these have rapidly enabled CVS to become, according to the *New York Times*, "arguably the country's biggest health care company, bigger than the drug makers and wholesalers, and bigger than the insurers."[171]

A SPEAR IN THE CHEST

Interface Carpets was already one of the biggest companies in its field when CEO Ray Anderson launched an ambitious program to guide his company to a sustainable business model. Anderson's visionary drive makes him one of my personal heroes.

Manufacturing carpet tiles for business offices, Interface, founded by Anderson in 1973, was a typical "take, make, waste" manufacturer and was, by all measures, a prosperous operation.

But in 1994, Anderson began to notice a persistent question from customers: "What was Interface doing for the environment?" Anderson realized that the answer was "nothing."

Then, preparing for a company presentation, he read the book *The Ecology of Commerce*[172] by Paul Hawken and had what he later referred to as a "spear in the chest epiphany."[173] He knew that it was his mission to transform the heavily petroleum-dependent company to one that would have zero negative environmental impact. That meant zero impact in terms of carbon footprint, water use, and waste. Ultimately, he hoped that the company would, in fact, have a positive impact on all those things.

Against dire predictions of failure, he put Interface on a 20-year program to produce products that were climate neutral, from the sourcing of materials to their useful life to their reclamation. He also pledged to modify all manufacturing, office, and distribution channels to attain the goal of zero waste and zero impact.

It was a hugely ambitious program, involving changing everything from the design of the products to sourcing of raw materials to manufacturing processes, water use, disposal of carpet after its useful life, and much more. Even something like an incorrect invoice was considered waste, because, in the final analysis, creating it, sending it, and correcting it required energy.

Sadly, Anderson passed away in 2011,[174] before the full realization of his ambitious vision. At Interface, energy use per unit of production is down 39 percent. Greenhouse gases are down by 82 percent. As of 2013, five of Interface's seven factories operated with 100 percent renewable electricity, and 35 percent of the company's total energy was generated from renewable sources.[175]

The list of Interface's successes is long and impressive, but more impressive still is this: since Anderson put Interface on the climb up what he dubbed "Mount Sustainability," output has grown by two-thirds, and Interface has become the largest manufacturer in its category.

THE EXAMINED LIFE

Patagonia, the athletic equipment and clothing manufacturer and retailer, although a private company, has a similar story. After learning about the environmental impact of the pesticides used in growing cotton, Patagonia went organic in 1996 and never looked back. Now, their commitment to environmentally and socially responsible behavior infuses every aspect of the company.

Specialists were hired to analyze working conditions and establish fair pay structures for every person who sews a Patagonia garment. As just one example of a very broad sustainability program, Patagonia manufactures its fleece jackets from recycled plastic bottles and then recycles used fleece jackets to make more of them. From using recycled paper to examining the fuel consumption of their employees as they commute to work to subsidizing childcare and much more, Patagonia strives to adhere to the highest standards of environmental and social corporate responsibility.[176]

In 2011 Patagonia decided to promote its position by encouraging customers to buy less. They took out a full page ad detailing the environmental costs of one of their top-selling sweaters. Its "worn-well program"[177] offers assistance to customers on how to repair tired and well-loved clothing. Customers are encouraged to share their stories on social media. This anti-growth strategy[178] may seem counterintuitive, but sales boomed by over 30 percent in the year following the campaign.

So much for skeptics who argue that renewable energy and sustainable resourcing are in opposition to profitable business practices. Environmental responsibility is neither a passing fad nor the whim of a few renegade CEOs. It's a business model.

There is a downside to running a company that strives for higher consciousness, however. "Living the examined life is a pain in the ass," according to company founder Yvon Chouinard as quoted on the company website.

Without question, manufacturing useful, quality products or offering a valuable service is difficult. It takes more effort to do it with care toward the environment and employees. Anything worth doing takes effort, and the previous examples prove that corporations, like individuals, can and should take full responsibility for manifesting their values in the world.

15

Time to Take Back Your Power

B uddhist teacher and writer Sangharakshita said, "Where you are is less important than whether or not you know where you are."

Like a stone cast into still water, ripples emanate outward from every action we take, from the food we eat to the clothes we wear, the way we power our homes, and the way our savings are invested. It's impossible to predict all of the ramifications of our impact on the financial ecosystem and the physical environment. What we do know is that finding our values and aligning our actions to create a better world from the inside out is the place to start.

As a country and as a planet, it's clear that we are out of balance, and it is clear why. The most powerful entities in the world, global corporations, have filled the power vacuum abdicated by their shareholders and are focused on short-term profit at the expense of everything and everyone else. As owners of these companies, we are complicit with them. But often we aren't even aware that we own them. Our savings, retirement plans, and pensions may hold companies that have policies and products directly in opposition to our most deeply held values.

That's why it is time to take back our power: to use new tools to understand what we own, to take a deep look inward and understand what really matters to us, our community, our families, our planet—to take ownership and actions to be part of the solution and hold corporations accountable.

Our empowerment can get us out of this quagmire by pushing corporations to transparently report their impact and make critical policy changes—to be accountable. As shareholders, it's our responsibility to push the companies that we own to embrace systemic change in areas ranging from diversity to human rights, energy, political spending, wealth disparity, and making healthy products. These changes have the potential to benefit employees, communities, customers, shareholders, and all stakeholders up and down the supply chain.

A generation or two from now, when our descendants look back on this era, they will say that this was the beginning of a new generation of corporate responsibility when the owners of the companies that were destroying the planet took back control and made balanced, long-term, sustainable growth the priority. We have strength in numbers, the legal right, and the moral obligation to exert our influence. We have the tools and access to information to look behind the curtain and band together as never before.

We are entering an era in which shareholders can and must shoulder our responsibility and unleash our power. I hope you will utilize the tools in this book and join the movement of shareholder advocates as we shape the world into a future that we desire.

Acknowledgments and Biographies of Interviewed Leaders

Acknowledgments

I want to thank the shareholder advocates that I have met and worked closely with over the past six years at As You Sow and especially those who agreed to be interviewed for this book and whose biographies are below. These are my colleagues, teachers, and mentors. These are the people who have spent their careers engaging corporations at the most fundamental level for change.

There are so many more leaders in the field that I did not have time or space to interview, but I stand on the shoulders of all of these people and have extreme gratitude for the work they do, for their tenacity, and for their belief in a just and abundant future.

I also want to thank Thomas Van Dyck, who introduced me to the idea that one person can be the change back in 1980 when we first met. He continues to be an inspiration for so many as he bridges finance and advocacy with empowerment. Also, I want to thank Conrad MacKerron, Senior VP at As You Sow, whose tenacity and dedication has led to many of the victories expressed in this book and who helped shape these pages. Deep gratitude goes to Danielle Fugere, who is my true partner in leadership at As You Sow.

Also thanks to so many others that enabled the writing of this book in many ways: Cari Rudd; Marianne Manilov; the entire staff of As You Sow, including Taraneh Arhamsadr, Kristin Costa, Patricia Jurewicz, Katie Levitt, Betsy MacMahon, Sarah Milne, Cody Mitcheltree, Andrew Montes, David Shugar, Amelia Timbers, Rosanna Landis Weaver, and Austin Wilson. And finally, deep thanks goes to my family, who support me with love and put up with my pointing out every problem that needs to be solved, and of course to my dogs, who have never trashed the neighborhood.

Biographies of Leaders Interviewed
(alphabetically by last name)

Father Michael Crosby[179] is a Catholic priest and member of the Midwest Capuchin Franciscans. He holds a Master's Degree in Economics and a PhD in Theology from the Graduate Theological Union in Berkeley, California. Father Crosby has been involved with the Interfaith Center on Corporate Responsibility, where he coordinates its tobacco engagements and is Executive Director of the Wisconsin, Iowa, and Minnesota Coalition for Responsible Investment, since 1973.

Randy Hayes has been described in the *Wall Street Journal* as "an environmental pit bull." He is Executive Director at Foundation Earth,[180] a new organization rethinking a human order that works within the planet's life support systems. As a former filmmaker and Rainforest Action Network[181] founder, he is a veteran of many high-visibility corporate accountability campaigns and has advocated for the rights of indigenous peoples. He served seven years as President of the City of San Francisco Commission on the Environment and as Director of Sustainability in the office of Oakland Mayor (now California governor) Jerry Brown. Hayes is a special advisor to the World Future Council.

Sanford J. Lewis is an attorney with over 30 years of experience in public policy–related issues, including environmental law, securities law, and public policy campaigns. He is a leading national expert on the filing and defense of shareholder proposals as well as corporate duties of disclosure of environmental and social issues in securities filings. He is also a documentary filmmaker. Lewis is a graduate of the University of Michigan Law School and holds a BS in Environmental Science and Urban Communications from Cook College, Rutgers University.

Conrad MacKerron has more than two decades of experience managing corporate dialogues and shareholder advocacy initiatives on cutting-edge social and environmental issues. Conrad founded the As You Sow Corporate Social Responsibility Program in 1997. He is a former senior social researcher at Piper Jaffray Philanthropic & Social Investment Consulting and Social Research Director at Progressive Asset Management (both social investment firms). He also served as Senior Analyst, Energy and Environment at the Investor Responsibility Research Center (now part of ISS). Formerly a journalist, he was Washington Bureau Chief for *Chemical Week* and a writer for BNA's *Environment Reporter*. He is author of *Business in the Rainforests: Corporations, Deforestation and Sustainability* (IRRC, 1993) and *Unlocking the Power of the Proxy* (2004). In 2007, he received the SRI Service Award from SIF for "outstanding contributions to the SRI community." MacKerron holds a Master's Degree in Journalism and Public Affairs from American University.

Nell Minow is Vice Chairman of ValueEdge Advisors,[183] which provides support for institutional investors on corporate governance and engagement initiatives. Previously, she was co-founder and board member of GMI Ratings, the LENS Fund, and Institutional Shareholder Services. Minow also worked as an attorney at EPA, OMB, and the Justice Department.

Sister Nora Nash is a Sister of St. Francis of Philadelphia and is the Director of Corporate Social Responsibility for her congregation. A member of the Philadelphia Coalition for Responsible Investment and the Interfaith Center on Corporate Responsibility (ICCR), she currently manages the congregation's assets in Community Development Loans and Social Justice Grants and is active in shareholder advocacy as a member of ICCR. Sister Nash has been recognized internationally for her work as a shareholder advocate.

Michael Passoff is CEO of Proxy Impact and has over 20 years experience in advancing corporate social responsibility. Previously he was Senior Program Director at As You Sow and has been involved in more than 300 corporate dialogues and resolutions on issues including energy, toxics, food safety, forestry, human rights and gender diversity. Listed as one of the "100 Most Influential People in Business Ethics" by *Ethisphere* magazine (2009), Passoff has also been co-winner of three Business Ethics Network Awards for shareholder campaigns and received the *Climate Change Business Journal*'s NGO Activist Award (2009)

William Patterson is founder of the 50/50 Board Responsibility Project and an Executive Director at CtW Investment Group. Previously, he was the Director of Office of Investment at American Federation of Labor and Congress of Industrial Organizations. He has served as co-chair of the Council of Institutional Investors and on the World Bank's Private Sector Advisory Group (PSAG) for the Global Corporate Governance Forum. In 2008, *Directorship* magazine named Patterson to the Directorship 100 as one of the most influential people in corporate governance.

Cari Rudd is an As You Sow board member and was chair of the Environmental Working Group for 11 years. Cari Rudd is a lifelong environmentalist as well as an investor and media expert. Active in politics for more than 20 years, she served as the executive director for Daschle Democrats and was the direct marketing advisor for the Democratic Senatorial Committee.

Tim Smith is the director of Environmental, Social, and Governance (ESG) shareowner engagement for Walden Asset Management.[184] Prior to joining the firm in 2000, Smith served as executive director of the Interfaith Center on Corporate Responsibility (ICCR) for 24 years. In 2007, 2012, and 2013, Smith was named as one of the "Top 100 Most Influential People in Business Ethics" by Ethisphere Institute. In 2011 and 2012, Smith was named one of the most influential people in corporate governance by the National Association of Corporate Directors.

Thomas Van Dyck has been a leader in the field of socially-responsible investing for more than 30 years. As managing director/financial advisor of the SRI Wealth Management Group at RBC Wealth Management*, he consults on $1.7 billion of ESG-screened assets. In 1992, he founded As You Sow, a shareholder advocacy organization, which engages corporations on environmental, human, and labor rights as well as corporate social responsibility initiatives. In 2014, Van Dyck was a featured guest on *Bill Moyers and Company* and discussed the Divest/Invest movement he helped initiate with his clients. In 2013, he was named one of the *Financial Times* Top 400 Financial Advisors. Van Dyck was also a featured speaker at the TedX Wall Street conference in 2012 and provided his expertise on ESG investing, which incorporates environmental, social, and governance factors in portfolio management to lower risks and improve returns. He graduated from Duke University in 1980 with a B.A. in Political Science. He is a member of the advisory board at Center for Social Entrepreneurship (CASE) at Duke University's Fuqua Business School. He is a Certified Investment Management Analyst (CIMA®) and holds his Series 7 and Series 66 FINRA licenses.

*RBC Wealth Management does not endorse or support As You Sow.

Links

The following resources can be downloaded at no cost.

Proxy Preview

- www.proxypreview.org

As You Sow Proxy Voting Guidelines

- http://www.asyousow.org/ays_report/proxy-voting-guidelines-2015/

Shareholder Resolution samples: these can be sorted by company/year/issue. All resolutions have full text, withdrawal letters, proxy memos, and other information available.

- http://www.asyousow.org/our-work/current-resolutions/
- http://www.ceres.org/investor-network/resolutions

A TEDx talk done by Thomas Van Dyck on sustainable investing is available on YouTube:

- https://www.youtube.com/watch?v=00Q3X0-Rihw

Company SEC filings can be found at:

- www.rankandfiled.com
- https://www.sec.gov/edgar/searchedgar/companysearch. html

Alliance Building for a Shareholder Movement

This book outlines ways that a dedicated individual with modest resources can participate in shareholder advocacy. However, many of the major wins on shareholder advocacy, from South Africa to the divestment movement on climate, were won because of a working alliance of organizations. It's important to seek to build a team of other investors or organizations and to be aware of and coordinate with other groups working on the same issues. While there is no one central coordinating point, there are several groups and resources you can check with if you go it alone to ensure you're not stepping on the toes of other shareholder advocates.

In addition, if you are a member of a national social change or environmental group, you can contact them to see if they are engaged in shareholder campaigns and to help organize and spread the word of those campaigns. If those groups are not engaged and you think there is a clear link between work the organization does and using the shareholder tool, you can also ask for meetings and advocate for those organizations to be involved in getting their members to take action as constituents and investors.

Your role in building a shareholder movement is not just to file shareholder actions. It is also to engage people in understanding that their investments matter and that they should be active shareholders.

You can engage others by:

1. Sharing the idea that everyone should understand what is in their portfolio.

2. Speaking at your local group or workplace on understanding how shareholders can have an impact.

3. Voting your shares on issues that matter and ask others to do the same.

4. Asking your investment advisor to screen your account and keep you informed.

One main issue to be aware of is, if you file a shareholder resolution with a company and it already has had a similar issue brought up, it can reject your proposal if it "substantially duplicates" another proposal that has already been submitted. If you see that a proposal has been filed in the area you are interested in, contact the filer and ask whether the issue was resolved and what their future filing plans are. Most likely they will welcome your support. There are several ways to determine this:

- *Proxy Preview* lists most environmental and social resolutions and is downloadable for free. You can search previous versions as far back as 2009. The Interfaith Center on Corporate Responsibility also publishes a proxy report with the full text of members' proposals; a fee is charged for this publication.

- The best way to make sure there has not been a previous filing on your topic is to review the company proxy statements for at least the past three years. These annual statements are easily accessible through the investor relations section of each public company's website, or through the SEC's EDGAR search tool.

- Many leading social investment firms who regularly file proposals list them on their websites. Firms who file often include (alphabetically) Arjuna Capital, Boston Common Asset Management, Calvert Investments, Christian Brothers Investments Services, Clean Yield Asset Management, Domini Social Investments, First Affirmative Financial Network, Green Century Funds, Harrington Investments, Jantz Management, Miller/Howard Investments, Newground Social Investment, Northstar Asset Management, Pax World Funds, Sonen Capital, Trillium Asset Management, Walden Asset Management, and Zevin Asset Management.

Glossary and Acronyms

AGM: Annual General Meeting. Publicly traded corporations are required by the Securities and Exchange Commission to hold a general meeting of shareholders to elect a board of directors, disclose financial information, and inform shareholders of past and future activities.

AUM: Assets Under Management. The market value of all assets managed on behalf of clients by a brokerage, mutual fund, venture capital fund, or other financial institution.

B-Corp: A private certification issued to for-profit companies by B Lab, a US-based non-profit organization. To be granted and to preserve certification, companies must receive a minimum score on an online assessment for social and environmental performance.

BP: British Petroleum, one of six major oil companies.

BPA: Bisphenol A, a chemical compound used to make certain plastics and epoxy resins used in common consumer goods, including water bottles, sports equipment, CDs, and DVDs, and as coatings inside water pipes, and food and beverage cans.

Board of Directors: In a publically traded corporation, a body elected by shareholders, which jointly oversees the activities of a company or organization.

CalPERS: California Public Employees' Retirement System is the largest pension fund in the United States.

CalSTRS: The California State Teachers' Retirement System.

CDC: Centers for Disease Control and Prevention.

CEO: Chief Executive Officer. The most senior corporate officer of a publicly traded corporation, reporting directly to the Board of Directors.

CERES: Coalition for Environmentally Responsible Economies, a leading advocacy organization for sustainability that convenes business, investors, and NGOs.

CFA: Certified Financial Analyst Institute is a global association of investment professionals that sets the standard for excellence in the industry.

CFC: Chlorofluorocarbons, a chemical used as spray propellant that impacted the ozone layer.

CII: Council of Institutional Investors is a nonprofit association of pension funds, other employee benefit funds, endowments, and foundations. It was established to be a leading voice for effective corporate governance.

CSR: Corporation Social Responsibility. Many companies now publish an annual CSR report and have professional CSR staff.

CU200: Short for the Carbon Underground 200. The list is based on the Carbon Tracker list of the 100 largest oil/gas and 100 largest coal companies as judged by reserves of fossil fuels.

DEF 14A: Short for "definitive," or final, proxy statement. "14A" refers to the fact that proxy statements are filed pursuant to Section 14(a) of the Securities Exchange Act of 1934.

EDGAR: The SEC's Electronic Data Gathering, Analysis, and Retrieval system. A database and data management system that performs automated collection, validation, indexing, acceptance, and forwarding of submissions by companies and others who are required by law to file forms with the SEC.

EFA: Educational Foundation of America, works to link its grant-making values with its investments to promote greater social responsibility of corporations. They seek to avoid investing in companies that contribute to the very problems they are attempting to address through grants.

EGA: Environmental Grantmakers Association works with members and partners to promote effective environmental philanthropy by sharing knowledge, fostering debate, cultivating leadership, facilitating collaboration, and catalyzing action.

EPK: Electronic Press Kit, like an analog one, only online and easily accessible to social media.

EPR: Extended Producer Responsibility is a strategy designed to promote the integration of environmental costs associated with goods throughout their life cycles into the market price of the products.

ERISA: Employee Retirement Income Security Act.

ESCRU: Episcopal Society for Cultural and Racial Unity, a faith-based organization that led the General Motors South African apartheid shareholder advocacy campaign.

ESG: Environmental, Social, and Governance, a generic term used in capital markets and by investors to evaluate corporate behavior and to determine the future financial performance of companies.

ETF: Exchange Traded Fund, a basket of companies that one can invest in that tracks an index and, unlike a mutual fund, can be traded at any time and generally has lower fees.

E-Waste: Short for electronic waste.

Form 8-K: The "current report" companies must file with the SEC to announce major events that shareholders should know about.

FTSE: Financial Times Stock Exchange

GHG: Greenhouse gas.

GICS: Global Industry Classification System.

GMO: Genetically Modified Organism, also known as a transgenic organism. Any organism whose genetic material has been altered using genetic engineering techniques. GMOs are the source of genetically modified foods and are also widely used in scientific research and to produce goods other than food.

ICCR: Interfaith Center on Corporate Responsibility, a coalition of more than 300 faith- and values-driven organizations that engage hundreds of multinational corporations annually to promote more sustainable and just practices.

IR: Investor Relations: A generic term for the department or individuals at a given public corporations office that attends to the needs of investors.

IRA: Individual Retirement Account is an account set up at a financial institution that allows an individual to save for retirement with tax-free growth or on a tax-deferred basis.

ISS: Institutional Shareholder Services, a proxy voting and analysis service.

Impact Investing: Investments "made into companies, organizations, and funds with the intention to generate a measurable, beneficial social or environmental impact alongside a financial return."

LGBT: Lesbian, Gay, Bisexual, and Transgender.

Material: In the context of corporate and securities law in the United States, a fact is defined as material if there is a substantial likelihood that a reasonable shareholder would consider it important in deciding how to vote their shares or invest their money.

MPAA: Motion Picture Association of America, the organization responsible for the classifications and ratings of all motion pictures exhibited and distributed commercially to the public in the United States.

NAV: Net Asset Value of a mutual fund at the end of a trading day.

NGO: A nongovernmental organization; neither a part of a government nor a conventional for-profit business. NGO activities might include advocating for human rights, environmental issues, or economic development. They are funded by governments, foundations, businesses, or private persons. In the United States, many NGOs are 501(c)(3) tax-exempt organizations.

No Action Letter: In the context of shareholder resolutions no-action letters describe the request, by a company to the SEC to analyze the particular facts and circumstances of a shareholder resolution to make a recommendation that the company can or cannot keep it off the proxy statement.

NRDC: Natural Respires Defense Council is a nonprofit that uses law, science, and the support of its 50,000+ members to protect the planet's wildlife and wild places and to ensure a safe, healthy planet.

Ordinary Business: Common practices, customs, and commercial activities that are necessary, normal, and incidental to a given business.

P/E: The ratio of a company's current share price compared to its per-share earnings, and used as a measure of value.

PET: Polyethylene Terephthalate is a form of polyester. It is extruded or molded into plastic bottles and containers for packaging foods and beverages, personal care products, and many other consumer products.

Proponent: A shareholder advocate who files the resolution is known as the proponent or lead filer.

Proxy: In the context of corporate law, a ballot cast by one person on behalf of another.

Proxy Access: A mechanism that gives shareowners the right to nominate directors for a corporate board.

Proxy Advisor: A firm hired by shareholders of public companies, in most cases an institutional investor of some type, to recommend and sometimes cast proxy statement votes on their behalf.

Proxy Impact: Helps foundations and socially responsible investors to align investments with values through ESG proxy voting and shareholder engagement services.

Proxy Statement: A written description of issues to be voted on by shareholders at a corporation's Annual General Meeting.

Proxy Voting Service: A group that analyzes issues in a corporation's proxy statement and votes on behalf of shareholders.

RDS: Royal Dutch Shell Corporation

ROI: Return on Investment. The return on an investment, divided by the cost of the investment, expressed as a percentage or a ratio. ROI is used to evaluate the efficiency of an investment or to compare a number of different investments.

S&P 500: Standard & Poor's 500 is an American stock market index based on the market capitalizations of the 500 largest companies that have common stock listed on the NYSE or NASDAQ.

SEC: The US Securities and Exchange Commission.

Shareholder resolution: Also called a proxy resolution or proposal, is submitted. by shareholders for a vote at the company's annual meeting. A shareholder resolution is generally not binding on the board and is advisory in nature.

Si2: Sustainable Investments Institute, a non-profit organization based in Washington, D.C., that conducts impartial research and publishes reports on organized efforts to influence corporate behavior on social and environmental issues.

SRI: Sustainable, Responsible, Impact investing. Formerly known as Socially Responsible Investment. An investment that is considered socially responsible because of the nature of the business the company conducts. It is closely aligned with ESG principles.

SWOP: Southwest Organizing Project was founded in 1980 by young activists of color to empower our communities in the Southwest to realize racial and gender equality and social and economic justice by bringing together the collective action, talents, and resources of the people within low-income communities of color to gain community control of land and resources.

UNPRI: United Nations Principles of Responsible Investing aims to help integrate consideration of environmental, social, and governance (ESG) issues by institutional investors into investment decision-making and ownership practices, and thereby improve long-term returns to beneficiaries.

VINIX: Vanguard Institutional Index Fund Institutional Shares.

About As You Sow

Founded in 1992, As You Sow is one of the nation's leading practitioners of corporate engagement and shareholder advocacy. It was founded on the belief that many environmental and human rights issues can be resolved by increased corporate responsibility, which is most effectively advanced through shareholder advocacy, coalition building, reports and benchmarking, and innovative legal strategies. The many companies whose policies and practices have been impacted by our work include ExxonMobil, Chevron, General Electric, McDonald's, Safeway, Whole Foods, Yum! Brands, Apple, Best Buy, Coca-Cola, Pepsi, Nestlé Waters, Starbucks, Target, Walt Disney, and DuPont.

In representing shareholders, As You Sow works directly with corporate executives and their teams, inviting them to co-create innovation across a series of issues. We build coalitions with investment community allies, including socially responsible investors, pension funds, labor groups, foundations, and faith-based investor communities. Through proactive dialogue, we educate and encourage companies to reform policies and practices by highlighting the financial risks of negative environmental and social actions and policies. If dialogue is insufficient in moving a company, we increase pressure by filing shareholder resolutions and reach out to institutional investors, media outlets, and proxy analysts to raise awareness and advocate for change. As You Sow has been able to help change corporations from the inside out. It is the corporations who are flexible, innovative, and responsive to both shareholders and consumers who thrive in the 21st century economy.

You can learn more at www.asyousow.org

About the Author

When Andrew was eight years old on a road trip with his parents, their car drove past a coal-fired power plant belching smoke into the sky. He asked his Dad, "Will the smoke ever fill up the sky?"

His dad laughed at the idea. "Oh, no, no!" he said.

"Why not?"

He shrugged. "It's just too big. It will never fill up."

Andrew accepted that answer. After all, he was just a child, and it was 1965.

Andrew has always been an environmentalist. Growing up near Long Island Sound, there were days when people could not go into the water because of pollution from a coal plant and industrial discharge in nearby Bridgeport. Also, the town landfill was right on the banks of the local river, flushing out to the Sound. The next town over located their dump literally on top of the wetlands, so with every tide, the runoff flowed out unabated.

There were warning signs not to eat the mussels that could be gathered at low tide, and fish die-offs were considered normal.

In 1980, living in New York City, he met Thomas Van Dyck through a mutual friend. They were fresh out of college, and Thomas enlisted him to join a coalition to stop the Indian Point nuclear reactor from receiving its license renewal. Thomas went on to become one of the founders of the socially responsible investing movement and founded As You Sow in 1992. Working to make the world a safer place was a deeply meaningful awakening for Andrew.

In 1989, with his wife and two-and-a-half-year-old son, he moved to Los Angeles. Andrew spent the next two decades raising a family and fighting several contentious local pollution and toxic chemical battles. Organizing neighborhood recycling programs, organizing protests over toxic pesticide spraying, and stopping a giant refuse company from creating a mega dump in a low-income community all gave Andrew a window into how to fight big business and where to find the leverage necessary to win.

In 2010 Andrew was hired as CEO of As You Sow and has seen firsthand the power of shareholder advocacy. In his travels he also observed that the vast majority of shareholders had no idea what corporate stocks they owned or how much power they had, which led to the writing of this book.

Endnotes

1 Long, Heather, "Over half of Americans have $0 in stocks," *CNN Money*, April 10, 2015, http://money.cnn.com/2015/04/10/investing/investing-52-percent-americans-have-no-money-in-stocks/

2 World Finance, "The Top Five Hostile Takeovers of all Time" http://www.worldfinance.com/strategy/the-top-five-hostile-takeovers-of-all-time

3 Ritholtz, Barry, "Where Have All the Public Companies Gone," Bloomberg View, June 24, 2015 http://www.bloombergview.com/articles/2015-06-24/where-have-all-the-publicly-traded-companies-gone-

4 Hayashi, Stuart K., "Progressivism: The Genesis of Eugenics"in *Hunting Down Social Darwinism: Will This Canard Go Extinct?* (Lanham, MD: Lexington Books, 2015) https://books.google.com/books?id=LjW_BgAAQBAJ&pg=PA104&lpg=PA104&dq=Brandeis+%E2%80%9CThere+is+no+such+thing+to+my+mind%E2%80%A6+as+an+innocent+stockholder&source=bl&ots=QZM_5WJH_3&sig=WuXhRFJKlrjkQ5vCtnjkW-7430Q&hl=en&sa=X&ved=0ahUKEwjQnvzR97PKAhVL9WMKHbSABF8Q6AEIJjAD#v=onepage&q=Brandeis%20%E2%80%9CThere%20is%20no%20

such%20thing%20to%20my%20mind%E2%80%A6%20
as%20an%20innocent%20stockholder&f=false (page 104)

5   Tracey S. Keys, Thomas W. Malnight and Christel K.
    Stoklund, "Corporate Clout 2013: Time for Responsible
    Capitalism," Strategy Dynamics Global SA, 2013. http://
    www.globaltrends.com/wp-content/uploads/2013/06/
    corporate%20clout%202013.pdf

6   Elizabeth Warren, "Elizabeth Warren: One Way to Rebuild
    Our Institutions," *New York Times*, January 29, 2016,
    http://www.nytimes.com/2016/01/29/opinion/elizabeth-
    warren-one-way-to-rebuild-our-institutions.html?
    smprod=nytcore-ipad&smid=nytcore-ipad-share

7   "McDonald's Pulls The Plug On Styrofoam,"
    SustainableBusiness.com, September 27, 2013, http://
    www.sustainablebusiness.com/index.cfm/go/news.display
    /id/25239

8   Holtz, Steve, "7-Eleven: Fourth-Largest Seller of Coffee
    in U.S.," *CSP Daily News*, February 20, 2013, http://www.
    cspnet.com/category-news/foodservice/articles/7-eleven-
    fourth-largest-seller-coffee-us

9   U.S. Department of Commerce: National Oceanic and
    Atmospheric Administration: National Ocean Service,
    "How Big is the 'Great Pacific Garbage Patch'? Science vs.
    Myth," U.S. Department of Commerce, http://response.
    restoration.noaa.gov/about/media/how-big-great-pacific-
    garbage-patch-science-vs-myth.html

10 Ivana Kottasova, "More Plastic than Fish in Oceans by
    2050," *CNN Money*, January 19, 2016, http://money.cnn.
    com/2016/01/19/news/economy/davos-plastic-ocean-fish/

11 "McDonald's (MCD)," YCharts, https://ycharts.com
    /companies/MCD/market_cap

12 "McDonald's Pulls the Plug on Styrofoam,"
    Sustainablebusiness.com, September 27, 2013, http://
    www.sustainablebusiness.com/index.cfm/go/news.display
    /id/25239

13 "SurfRider Foundation" home page, https://www.surfrider. org/

14 For a full list of the CA ordinances see SurfRider Foundation, Plastics Pollution: http://www.surfrider.org /pages/polystyrene-ordinances_

15 "Sustainable Investing: Establishing Long-Term Value and Performance" Mark Fulton, Bruce Kahn and Camilia Sharpies. Page 5 https://institutional.deutscheam.com /content/_media/Sustainable_Investing_2012.pdf

16 "Socially Responsible Investing: Delivering Competitive Performance," Lei Liao and Jim Campagna, TIAA-CREF Asset Management, Sept 2014 (page 1) https://www.tiaa. org/public/pdf/C19224_SRI_White_Paper_v13.pdf

17 CalPERS, "'CalPERS Effect' Continues to Improve Company Performance," Online, https://www.calpers. ca.gov/page/newsroom/calpers-news/2014/company-performance

18 "ESG Issues in Investing: Investors Debunk the Myths," CFA Institute, 2015, http://irrcinstitute.org/pdf/FINAL-Fact-Sheet-ESG-Survey-August-2015.pdf

19 https://www.msci.com/resources/factsheets/index_fact_ sheet/msci-kld-400-social-index.pdf

20 Kenneth C. Levine and Peter J. Sherman, "Ten Simple Principles for Treating Employees as Assets," *Quality Digest*, July 26, 2010, http://www.qualitydigest.com/inside/quality-insider-column/ten-simple-principles-treating-employees-assets.html#

21 "The Six Principles," Principles for Responsible Investment, http://www.unpri.org/about-pri/the-six-principles/

22 "The Ceres Principles," Ceres, http://www.ceres.org/about-us/our-history/ceres-principles

23 Marshall.edu, "The Sullivan Principles," Online, http:// www.marshall.edu/revleonsullivan/principles.htm

24   Answers.com, "Who said, "When the people lead the leaders will follow?" Online, http://www.answers.com/Q /Who_said_When_the_people_lead_the_leaders_will_ follow

25   Wikipedia, "Montreal Protocol," Online, https:// en.wikipedia.org/wiki/Montreal_Protocol

26   Brian Handwerk, "Whatever Happened to the Ozone Hole?" *National Geographic*, May 7, 2010, http://news. nationalgeographic.com/news/2010/05/100505-science-environment-ozone-hole-25-years/

27   Arthur Neslen, "Islamic Leaders Issue Bold Call for Rapid Phase out of Fossil Fuels," *The Guardian*, August 18, 2015, http://www.theguardian.com/environment/2015/aug/18 /islamic-leaders-issue-bold-call-rapid-phase-out-fossil-fuels?CMP=share_btn_tw

28   University of California, San Francisco, "Stanton Glantz, PhD," Online, https://tobacco.ucsf.edu/users/sglantz

29   LinkedIn, "Gina Intinarelli RN MS PhD," Online, https:// www.linkedin.com/in/gina-intinarelli-rn-ms-phd-b42a749 9?authType=name&authToken=hD8F

30   University of California, San Francisco, "Smoke Free Movies," Online, http://smokefreemovies.ucsf.edu/

31   World Health Organization, *Smoke-Free Movies: From Evidence to Action* (Geneva, Switzerland: WHO Press, 2011)   http://apps.who.int/iris/bitstream/10665/44730/1 /9789241502399_eng.pdf

32   "Unlocking the Power of the Proxy," As You Sow, http:// www.asyousow.org/ays_report/unlocking-the-power-of-the-proxy/

33   https://www.law.cornell.edu/cfr/text/17/240.14a-8

34   http://www.asyousow.org/ays_report/proxy-voting-guidelines-2016/

35   "Proxy Preview," http://www.proxypreview.org/

36   "ISS," http://www.issgovernance.com/governance-solutions /proxy-voting-services/

37 "Glass Lewis," http://www.glasslewis.com/

38 "Egan-Jones Proxy Services," http://www.ejproxy.com/

39 "Proxy Impact," http://proxyimpact.com/

40 "Mutual Fund," Investopedia, http://www.investopedia.
    com/terms/m/mutualfund.asp

41 "Money Manager," Investopedia, http://www.investopedia.
    com/terms/m/moneymanager.asp

42 "Prospectus," Investopedia, http://www.investopedia.com
    /terms/p/prospectus.asp

43 "ETF," Investopedia, http://www.investopedia.com/terms/e
    /etf.asp

44 "Index Fund," Investopedia, http://www.investopedia.com
    /terms/i/indexfund.asp

45 "Diversification," Investopedia, http://www.investopedia.
    com/terms/d/diversification.asp

46 Bach, Betsy/Piper, "ERISA Plans: What is Your Fiduciary
    Responsibility?" IMCA, https://www.imca.org/sites
    /default/files/current-issues/Whitepapers/2013WP_
    ERISAPlans.pdf

47 "New Spotlight on Proxy Voting," PlanSponsor, November
    1994, http://www.plansponsor.com/MagazineArticle.
    aspx?id=6442462506

48 "Proxy Democracy," http://proxydemocracy.org/

49 Schwartz, John, "Norway Will Divest From Coal in Push
    Against Climate Change," *New York Times*, June 5, 2015,
    http://www.nytimes.com/2015/06/06/science/norway-
    in-push-against-climate-change-will-divest-from-coal.
    html?_r=0

50 Investopedia, "share class", http://www.investopedia.com
    /terms/s/share_class.asp

51 "Sustainable Investments Institute," http://www.siinstitute.org/

52 "Proxy Impact," http://proxyimpact.com/

53 Rank and filed, http://rankandfiled.com/#/

54 "EDGAR,"Wikipedia, April 20, 2016, https://en.wikipedia.
    org/wiki/EDGAR

55 "EDGAR: Company Filings" U.S. Securities and Exchange
    Commission,   https://www.sec.gov/edgar/searchedgar
    /companysearch.html

56 "Resolutions," As You Sow, http://www.asyousow.org/our-
    work/current-resolutions/

57 http://www.ceres.org/investor-network/resolutions

58 "The Kroger Co," United States Securities and Exchange
    Commission,   https://www.sec.gov/Archives/edgar/data
    /56873/000120677415001665/kroger_def14a.htm

59 Vedantam, Shankar, "Is Arguing with Passion The Most
    Effective Way to Persuade Opponents?" NPR, December
    17, 2015, http://www.npr.org/2015/12/17/460082538/is-
    arguing-with-passion-the-most-effective-way-to-persuade-
    opponents

60 Willer, Robb and Matthew Feinberg, "Political Persuasion,"
    New York Times, November 13, 2015, http://www.nytimes.
    com/2015/11/15/opinion/sunday/the-key-to-political-
    persuasion.html?_r=0

61 Cabraal, Amal, "The Value of Corporate Branding 'The
    Unilever Story,'" SuperBrands.com, August 2008, http://
    www.superbrands.com/lkc1/presentation/amal_cabraal_
    presentation.pdf

62 As reported in Waste News, May 14, 2007 page 22

63 "Basel Action Network," http://www.ban.org/

64 As reported in Waste News, May 14, 2007 page 22

65 "Materiality: Why Is It Important?" Sustainability
    Accounting   Standards   Board,   http://www.sasb.org
    /materiality/important/

66 Sustainability Accounting Standards Board, materiality by
    industry, http://using.sasb.org/

67 *TSC Industries, Inc. v. Northway, Inc.* 426 U.S. 438 (1976)," Justia US Supreme Court, June 14, 1976, https://supreme. justia.com/cases/federal/us/426/438/case.html

68 Park, Doug, "3 Myths About SASB and Materiality," Sustainable Accounting Standards Board, November 5, 2013, http://www.sasb.org/3-myths-sasb-materiality/

69 Bainbridge, Stephen, "Revitalizing SEC Rule 14a-8's Ordinary Business Exemption: Preventing Shareholder Micromanagement by Proposal," ProfessorBainbridge. com, March 18, 2016, http://www.professorbainbridge. com/professorbainbridgecom/2016/03/revitalizing-sec-rule-14a-8s-ordinary-business-exemption-preventing-shareholder-micromanagement-by-p.html

70 "Shareholders Applaud CVS Caremark's Decision to End Tobacco Sales," Interfaith Center on Corporate Responsibility, February 5, 2014, http://www.iccr.org /shareholders-applaud-cvs-caremark%E2%80%99s-decision-end-tobacco-sales

71 Greene, Michael, "Wal-Mart's Holder Says District Court Was Right to Reverse SEC on Gun Resolution," *Bloomberg BNA*, February 6, 2015, http://www.bna.com/walmart-sholder-says-n17179922826/

72 Stempel, Jonathan, "Wal-Mart Defeats Bid for Shareholder Vote on Gun Sales," *Reuters*, April 14, 2015, http://www. reuters.com/article/us-walmart-trinitychurch-lawsuit-guns-idUSKBN0N52DR20150414

73 "Filings & Forms," U.S. Securities and Exchange Commission, https://www.sec.gov/edgar.shtml

74 "EDGAR," Wikipedia, https://en.wikipedia.org/wiki /EDGAR

75 "SEC Adopts Rules for Say-on-Pay and Golden Parachute Compensation as Required Under Dodd-Frank Act," U.S. Securities and Exchange Commission, January 25, 2011, https://www.sec.gov/news/press/2011/2011-25.htm

76 Hyatt, James, "Business Groups Sue to Block Proxy Access," business-ethics.com, September 29, 2010, http://business-ethics.com/2010/09/29/1336-u-s-chamber-business-roundtable-challenge-proxy-access-in-court/

77 Leaton, James, "*Carbon Bubble,*" Carbon Tracker Initiative, http://www.carbontracker.org/report/carbon-bubble/

78 http://www.asyousow.org/wp-content/uploads/2013/07/2013-consol-reso.pdf

79 Fleming, Peyton, "Investors Ask Fossil Fuel Companies to Assess How Business Plans Fare in Low-carbon Future," Ceres, October 24, 2013, http://www.ceres.org/press/press-releases/investors-ask-fossil-fuel-companies-to-assess-how-business-plans-fare-in-low-carbon-future

80 "Silent Spring," Wikipedia, https://en.wikipedia.org/wiki/Silent_Spring

81 "The History of Earth Day," earthday.org, http://www.earthday.org/earth-day-history-movement

82 "Smoking in the Movies," Center for Disease Control and Prevention, http://www.cdc.gov/tobacco/data_statistics/fact_sheets/youth_data/movies/

83 "Occupy Wall Street," Wikipedia, https://en.wikipedia.org/wiki/Occupy_Wall_Street

84 "Movie Mom," beliefnet.com, http://www.beliefnet.com/columnists/moviemom/

85 Hurtado, Patricia, *Bloomberg Quicktake*, February 23, 2016, http://www.bloombergview.com/quicktake/the-london-whale

86 Hurtado, Patricia, *Bloomberg Quicktake*, February 23, 2016, http://www.bloombergview.com/quicktake/the-london-whale

87 "Chronology," Bay Area Coalition for Headwaters, http://headwaterspreserve.org/headwaters-forest-campaign-history/

88 "Friends of Clayoquot Sound," http://focs.ca/

89 "Bay   Area   Coalition   for   Headwaters,"   http://
    headwaterspreserve.org/

90 "Environmental Protection Information Center," http://
    www.wildcalifornia.org/

91 "Trees Foundation," https://go.treesfoundation.org/

92 "Sierra Club," http://sierraclub.org/

93 "Rainforest Action Network," http://www.ran.org/

94   "Greenpeace," http://www.greenpeace.org/usa/

95 "Rose Foundation," http://rosefdn.org/

96 "About Luna,"Julia Butterfly Hill, http://www.juliabutterfly.
    com/about-luna.html

97 Forests For All Forever, https://us.fsc.org/en-us

98 Hornblower, Margaret, "Next Stop, Home Depot," *Time*,
    June 24, 2001, http://content.time.com/time/magazine
    /article/0,9171,140221,00.html

99 Cabraal, Amal, "The Value of Corporate Brandind 'The
    Unilever Story,'" superbrands.com, August 2008,

100 Muller, Mike, *"The Baby Killer,"* War on Want, London,
    England, March 1974, http://archive.babymilkaction.org
    /pdfs/babykiller.pdf

101 Charles Piller, Edmund Sanders and Robyn Dixon, "Dark
    Cloud over Good Works of Gates Foundation" http://www.
    latimes.com/news/la-na-gatesx07jan07-story.html January
    7, 2007

102 Rachel's Network main page, http://rachelsnetwork.org/

103 Kopicki, Allison, "Strong Support for Labeling Modified
    Foods," *New York Times*, July 27, 2013, http://www.nytimes.
    com/2013/07/28/science/strong-support-for-labeling-
    modified-foods.html?_r=0

104 http://www.asyousow.org/wp-content/uploads/2013/07
    /2013-abbott-reso.pdf

105 http://www.asyousow.org/wp-content/uploads/2013/07
    /2013-abbott-reso.pdf

106 Strom, Stephanie, "Similac Advance Infant Formula to Be Offered G.M.O.-Free," *New York Times*, May 25, 2015, http://www.nytimes.com/2015/05/26/business/similac-advance-infant-formula-to-be-offered-gmo-free.html?_r=0

107 Brait, Ellen, "Portland's Bridge-hangers and 'Kayaktivists' Claim Win in Shell Protest ," *The Guardian*, July 31, 2015, http://www.theguardian.com/business/2015/jul/31/portland-bridge-shell-protest-kayaktivists-fennica-reaction

108 Olstad, Rebekah, "Kayaktivists Say 'Shell No!' to Arctic Drilling," *Earthjustice*, July 21, 2015, http://earthjustice.org/blog/2015-july/kayaktivists-say-shell-no-to-arctic-drilling

109 http://www.asyousow.org/wp-content/uploads/2014/03/exxonmobil2014carbonbubble.pdf

110 http://www.asyousow.org/wp-content/uploads/2014/04/exxonmobil2014carbonbubble_withdrawal.pdf

111 http://www.asyousow.org/wp-content/uploads/2014/05/ExxonMobil-Response-to-As-You-Sow-20140331.pdf

112 Cardwell, Diane, "In Shift, Exxon Mobil to Report on Risks to Its Fossil Fuel Assets," *New York Times*, March 20, 2014, http://www.asyousow.org/wp-content/uploads/2014/04/20140320-newyorktimes-in_shift_exxon_mobil_to_report_on_risks_to_its_fossil_fuel_assets.pdf

113 Davis, Alyssa and Lawrence Mishel, "CEO Pay Continues to Rise as Typical Workers Are Paid Less," *Economic Policy Institute*, June 12, 2014, http://www.epi.org/publication/ceo-pay-continues-to-rise/

114 "CEO Pay," As You Sow, http://ceopay.asyousow.org/

115 "Richest 1% will own more than all the rest by 2016," Oxfam International, January 19, 2015, https://www.oxfam.org/en/pressroom/pressreleases/2015-01-19/richest-1-will-own-more-all-rest-2016

116 Giammona, Craig, "McDonald's to Increase Hourly Wages, Offer Paid Vacation," *Bloomberg*, April 1, 2015, http://www.

bloomberg.com/news/articles/2015-04-01/mcdonald-s-will-raise-worker-pay-by-more-than-10-journal-says

117 Boak, Josh, "Despite the Raises, Many Wal-Mart Workers Still Fall Below 'Living Wage,'" *Portland Press Herald*, February 19, 2015 http://www.pressherald.com/2015/02/19/despite-the-raises-many-wal-mart-workers-still-fall-below-living-wage/

118 Levy, Gabrielle, "How Citizens United Has Changed Politics in 5 Years," *US News & World Report*, January 21, 2015, http://www.usnews.com/news/articles/2015/01/21/5-years-later-citizens-united-has-remade-us-politics

119 "Center for Political Accountability," http://politicalaccountability.net/

120 Morgenson, Gretchen, "In Whole Foods Backlash, a Chance to Air Out Stagnant Boardrooms," *New York Times*, February 21, 2015, http://www.nytimes.com/2015/02/22/business/in-whole-foods-backlash-a-chance-to-air-out-stagnant-boardrooms.html

121 Myatt, Mike "Boards Remain Pale, Male and Stale—Old Boys' Club Alive And Well," *Forbes*, September 19, 2013, http://www.forbes.com/sites/mikemyatt/2013/09/19/boards-remain-pale-male-and-stale-old-boys-club-alive-and-well/

122 Miller, Claire Cain, "Women on the Board: Quotas Have Limited Success," *New York Times*, June 19, 2014, http://www.nytimes.com/2014/06/20/upshot/women-on-the-board-quotas-have-limited-success.html

123 Credit Suisse Research Institute, "Gender Diversity and Corporate Performance," August 2012, https://c4mb.wordpress.com/2012/09/22/credit-suisse-research-institute-report-gender-diversity-and-corporate-performance/

124 Myatt, Mike, "Top 10 Reasons Diversity is Good for the Boardroom," *Forbes*, November 18, 2013, http://www.forbes.com/sites/mikemyatt/2013/11/18/top-10-reasons-diversity-is-good-for-the-boardroom/#461347645fda

125 Thirty Percent Coalition for Gender Diverse Boardrooms, http://www.30percentcoalition.org

126 Stifel Financial Board Diversity 2016 Shareholder Resolution, http://www.trilliuminvest.com/shareholder-proposal/stifel-financial-board-diversity-2016/

127 Carbon Disclosure Project, https://www.cdp.net/en-US /Pages/HomePage.aspx

128 http://www.asyousow.org/media-center/reports/?program= &ays_year=&initiative=consumer-packaging&keyword=

129 "Slipping Through the Cracks: An Issue Brief on Nanomaterials in Foods," As You Sow, http://www. asyousow.org/ays_report/slipping-through-the-cracks/

130 "Seeking Safer Packaging: Ranking Packaged Food Companies on BPA," As You Sow, http://www.asyousow. org/ays_report/seeking-safer-packaging-ranking-packaged-food-companies-on-bpa-2010/

131 "Disclosing the Facts: Transparency and Risk in Hydraulic Fracturing," As You Sow, http://disclosingthefacts.org /report/

132 Governance & Accountability Institute, Inc, FLASH REPORT - Seventy-Five Percent (75%) of the S&P 500 Index Published Corporate Sustainability Reports in 2014 http://www.ga-institute.com/nc/issue-master-system/news-details/npage/1/article/flash-report-seventy-five-percent-75-of-the-sp-index-published-corporate-sustainability-rep.html

133 Ceres History, Sustainability Reporting: Ceres Catalyzes a Worldwide Movement, http://www.ceres.org/about-us /our-history/sustainability-reporting-ceres-catalyzes-a-worldwide-movement

134 "Product Stewardship and Extended Producer Responsibility (EPR)," CalRecycle, http://www.calrecycle. ca.gov/epr/

135 "Extended Producer Responsibility," OECD, http://www.oecd.org/env/tools-evaluation /extendedproducerresponsibility.htm

136 McKibben, Bill, "Global Warming's Terrifying New Math," *Rolling Stone*, http://www.rollingstone.com/politics/news/global-warmings-terrifying-new-math-20120719

137 "Do the Math," 350.org, http://math.350.org/

138 "Hip Hop Caucus" Rev. Lennox Yearwood Jr. http://www.hiphopcaucus.org/our-story/team?catid=5&id=5:rev-yearwood

139 "Green Faith" Rev. Fletcher Harper, http://www.greenfaith.org/about/staff

140 "Healthcare without Harm," Gary Cohen, https://noharm-uscanada.org/sites/default/files/documents-files/2654/gary_cohen_biography.pdf

141 "Divest-Invest Philanthropy," http://divestinvest.org/philanthropy/

142 "Divest-Invest Philanthropy," http://divestinvest.org/philanthropy/

143 Arabella Advisors, Measuring the Growth of the Global Fossil Fuel Divestment and Clean Energy Investment Movements, http://www.arabellaadvisors.com/wp-content/uploads/2015/09/Measuring-the-Growth-of-the-Divestment-Movement.pdf

144 Schwartz, Jon, "Rockefellers, Heirs to an Oil Fortune, Will Divest Charity of Fossil Fuels,"The New York Times, September 21, 2014, http://www.nytimes.com/2014/09/22/us/heirs-to-an-oil-fortune-join-the-divestment-drive.html?_r=0

145 Lapin, Lisa, "Stanford to Divest from Coal Companies," May 6, 2014, http://news.stanford.edu/news/2014/may/divest-coal-trustees-050714.html

146 Schwartz, John, "Norway Will Divest from Coal in Push against Climate Change," *New York Times*, June 5, 2015, http://www.nytimes.com/2015/06/06/science/norway-in-push-against-climate-change-will-divest-from-coal.html?_r=0

147 "Institutions Worth $2.6 Trillion Have Now Pulled Investments out of Fossil Fuels," *The Guardian*, http://www.theguardian.com/environment/2015/sep/22/leonardo-dicaprio-joins-26tn-fossil-fuel-divestment-movement

148 350.org, "Divestment Commitments Pass the $3.4 Trillion Mark at COP 21," http://350.org/cop21-divestment/

149 "Market Vectors-Coal ETF," Market Watch, http://www.marketwatch.com/investing/fund/kol

150 Crowe, Tyler, "How Long Can Big Oil Keep Its Dividends With $30 Oil," The Motley Fool, January 15, 2016, http://www.fool.com/investing/general/2016/01/15/how-long-can-big-oil-keep-its-dividends-at-30-oil.aspx

151 "Exxon Mobil's Dividend Could Be in Danger," Seeking Alpha, February 22, 2016, http://seekingalpha.com/article/3917056-exxon-mobils-dividend-danger

152 Hulac, Benjamin, "Influential Financiers Making Their Own Moves to Divest from Some Fossil Fuels," E&E Publishing LLC, February 19, 2015, http://www.eenews.net/stories/1060013659

153 "Laudato Si" Encyclical Letter of the Holy Father, Pope Francis, http://w2.vatican.va/content/francesco/en/encyclicals/documents/papa-francesco_20150524_enciclica-laudato-si.html

154 "Yale to Partially Divest from Fossil Fuels," Yale Daily News, http://yaledailynews.com/blog/2016/04/12/yale-begins-divestment-from-fossil-fuels/

155 "Citi Announces $100 Billion, 10-Year Commitment to Finance Sustainable Growth," CitiGroup, February 18, 2015, http://www.citigroup.com/citi/news/2015/150218a.htm

156 http://divestinvest.org/individual/

157 https://fossilfreefunds.org

158 "United Nations Framework Convention on Climate Change,"Wikipedia,https://en.wikipedia.org/wiki/United_Nations_Framework_Convention_on_Climate_Change

159 Kolbert, Elizabeth, "The Weight of the World," *New Yorker*, August 24, 2015, http://www.newyorker.com/ magazine/2015/08/24/the-weight-of-the-world

160 Nussbaum, Alex, "Fossil-Fuel Divestment Tops $3.4 Trillian Mark, Activists Say," *Bloomberg*, December 2, 2015, http://www.bloomberg.com/news/articles/2015-12-02 /fossil-fuel-divestment-tops-3-4-trillion-mark-activists-say

161 "Divest-Invest Philanthropy," http://divestinvest.org/wp-content/uploads/2015/12/12.5_Divest-Invest%20Brief_ FINAL.pdf

162 "Divest-Invest Individual," http://divestinvest.org/individual/

163 "Divest-Invest Individual," http://divestinvest.org/individual/

164 "HIP Investor," http://hipinvestor.com/

165 "Socially Responsible Retirement," https://socialk.com/

166 "Green + Retirement," Green Retirement, http://www. greenretirement.com/greenretirement.aspx

167 "What Is the Difference between a 401(k) Plan and a 403(b) Plan?" Investopedia, http://www.investopedia.com /ask/answers/100314/what-difference-between-401k-plan-and-403b-plan.asp

168 Enskog, Dorothee, *"Women's Positive Impact on Corporate Engagement,"* Credit Suisse, September 23, 2014, https:// www.credit-suisse.com/us/en/news-and-expertise/investing /articles/news-and-expertise/2014/09/en/womens-impact-on-corporate-performance-letting-the-data-speak.html

169 http://www.ussif.org/

170 Gelles, David, "At Aetna, a C.E.O.'s Management by Mantra," *New York Times*, February 27, 2015, http:// www.nytimes.com/2015/03/01/business/at-aetna-a-ceos-management-by-mantra.html?_r=0

171 Tabuchi, Hiroko, "How CVS Quit Smoking and Grew Into a Health Care Giant," *New York Times*, July 11, 2015, http://www.nytimes.com/2015/07/12/business/how-cvs-quit-smoking-and-grew-into-a-health-care-giant. html?smprod=nytcore-ipad&smid=nytcore-ipad-share

172   Hawken, Paul, *The Ecology of Commerce Revised Edition: A Declaration of Sustainability*, Collins Business Essentials, New York, NY: October 26, 2010. http://www.amazon. com/Ecology-Commerce-Revised-Edition-Sustainability /dp/0061252794

173   Gordan, Paula, "Ray Anderson: a Spear in the Chest." YouTube video, 1:41. Posted February 2, 2010. https://www. youtube.com/watch?v=9SpX73qhFq8

174   Mason, Peter, "Ray Anderson Obituary," *The Guardian*, August 26, 2011, http://www.theguardian.com /environment/2011/aug/26/ray-anderson-obituary

175   http://www.interfaceglobal.com/sustainability.aspx

176   Spivey, Sara, "How Patagonia Is Using Cause Marketing to Define Their Brand and Drive Sales," Bazaar Voice, July 7, 2015, http://blog.bazaarvoice.com/2015/07/07 /how-patagonia-is-using-cause-marketing-to-define-their-brand-and-drive-sales/

177   Vogl, Eileen, "What Patagonia Learned on Its Worn Wear Mobile Repair Tour," brand channel, May 21, 2015, http://brandchannel.com/2015/05/21/patagonia-worn-wear-052015/

178   MacKinnon, J.B., "Patagonia's Anti-Growth Strategy," *New Yorker*, May 21, 2015, http://www.newyorker.com /business/currency/patagonias-anti-growth-strategy

179   "Michael Crosby," MichaelCrosby.net, www.michaelcrosby. net

180   "Foundation Earth," http://www.fdnearth.org/

181   "Rainforest Action Network," http://www.ran.org/

182   "Invoking the Pause," http://www.invokingthepause.org/

183   "Value Edge Advisors," www.valuedgeadvisors.com

184   "Walden Asset Management," http://www. waldenassetmgmt.com/

Index

Berrett–Koehler
Publishers

Berrett-Koehler is an independent publisher dedicated to an ambitious mission: *connecting people and ideas to create a world that works for all.*

We believe that to truly create a better world, action is needed at all levels—individual, organizational, and societal. At the individual level, our publications help people align their lives with their values and with their aspirations for a better world. At the organizational level, our publications promote progressive leadership and management practices, socially responsible approaches to business, and humane and effective organizations. At the societal level, our publications advance social and economic justice, shared prosperity, sustainability, and new solutions to national and global issues.

A major theme of our publications is "Opening Up New Space." Berrett-Koehler titles challenge conventional thinking, introduce new ideas, and foster positive change. Their common quest is changing the underlying beliefs, mindsets, institutions, and structures that keep generating the same cycles of problems, no matter who our leaders are or what improvement programs we adopt.

We strive to practice what we preach—to operate our publishing company in line with the ideas in our books. At the core of our approach is stewardship, which we define as a deep sense of responsibility to administer the company for the benefit of all of our "stakeholder" groups: authors, customers, employees, investors, service providers, and the communities and environment around us.

We are grateful to the thousands of readers, authors, and other friends of the company who consider themselves to be part of the "BK Community." We hope that you, too, will join us in our mission.

A BK Currents Book

This book is part of our BK Currents series. BK Currents books advance social and economic justice by exploring the critical intersections between business and society. Offering a unique combination of thoughtful analysis and progressive alternatives, BK Currents books promote positive change at the national and global levels. To find out more, visit **www.bkconnection.com**.

Berrett–Koehler
Publishers

Connecting people and ideas
to create a world that works for all

Dear Reader,

Thank you for picking up this book and joining our worldwide community of Berrett-Koehler readers. We share ideas that bring positive change into people's lives, organizations, and society.

To welcome you, we'd like to offer you a free e-book. You can pick from among twelve of our bestselling books by entering the promotional code **BKP92E** here: http://www.bkconnection.com/welcome.

When you claim your free e-book, we'll also send you a copy of our e-newsletter, the *BK Communiqué*. Although you're free to unsubscribe, there are many benefits to sticking around. In every issue of our newsletter you'll find

- A free e-book
- Tips from famous authors
- Discounts on spotlight titles
- Hilarious insider publishing news
- A chance to win a prize for answering a riddle

Best of all, our readers tell us, "Your newsletter is the only one I actually read." So claim your gift today, and please stay in touch!

Sincerely,

Charlotte Ashlock
Steward of the BK Website

Questions? Comments? Contact me at bkcommunity@bkpub.com.

MIX
Paper from
responsible sources
FSC® C002589

Certified

Corporation
bcorporation.net